Submerged Soils

NIPA® GENX ELECTRONIC RESOURCES & SOLUTIONS P. LTD.
New Delhi-110 034

About the Author

Dr. Anandkumar Naorem, currently employed as a scientist at ICAR-Central Arid Zone Research Institute in Jodhpur, India, previously held the position of Head-in-charge at ICAR-CAZRI, RRS-Bhuj, India. He completed his bachelor's degree at Assam Agricultural University, Assam, India, and pursued his master's degree in soil microbiology and bioformulation at the College of Post-Graduate Studies, Central Agricultural University, Meghalaya, India. His doctoral research, conducted at Bidhan Chandra Krishi Viswavidyalaya in West Bengal, India, focused on the remediation of soil heavy metals for safer crop cultivation.

Dr. Naorem, who has authored several national and international publications, has received national recognition, including the 2015 Best Zonal Master's Thesis award from the Indian Society of Soil Science and the UGC-Maulana Azad National Fellowship for Minority Students (India). He is acknowledged for his contributions as a young scientist by numerous societies and organizations, having led various research projects on soil quality in arid regions, studies on elevated carbon dioxide levels, and investigations into halophytes. Notably, he has played a key role in international initiatives promoting spineless cactus as a dryland feed option in Gujarat.

The Professional's Notes Series

Volume 04

Submerged Soils

Anandkumar Naorem
Scientist, Division of IFS
ICAR-Central Arid Zone Research Institute
Ministry of A&Fw, Government of India
Jodhpur-342003, Rajasthan, India

NIPA® GENX ELECTRONIC RESOURCES & SOLUTIONS P. LTD.
New Delhi-110 034

NIPA® GENX ELECTRONIC RESOURCES & SOLUTIONS P. LTD.

101,103, Vikas Surya Plaza, CU Block
L.S.C.Market, Pitam Pura, New Delhi-110 034
Ph : +91 11 27341616, 27341717, 27341718
E-mail: newindiapublishingagency@gmail.com
www: www.nipabooks.com

For customer assistance, please contact
Phone: + 91-11-27 34 17 17
Fax: + 91-11- 27 34 16 16
E-Mail: feedbacks@nipabooks.com

Print ISBN: 978-93-58875-23-2

ebook ISBN: 978-93-58873-22-1

Composed and Designed by NIPA®.

Preface

Welcome to Volume 04, dedicated to the fascinating realm of "Submerged Soils." In this volume, we are on an exploration of the unique characteristics, ecological dynamics, and management challenges associated with soils subjected to waterlogging and submersion. Submerged soils, often overlooked in traditional soil science literature, represent a diverse and dynamic ecosystem shaped by the presence of water. From wetlands and floodplains to rice paddies and riparian zones, these submerged environments play crucial roles in regulating water flow, nutrient cycling, and biodiversity. In this volume, we delve into the intricacies of submerged soils, shedding light on their ecological functions, management strategies, and the implications for sustainable land use.

Understanding the characteristics and behaviour of submerged soils is essential for managing these ecosystems effectively and mitigating the impacts of waterlogging and submersion. By examining the physical, chemical, and biological properties of submerged soils, we gain insights into their resilience, adaptability, and ecological significance. Moreover, we explore the management practices and restoration techniques that can be employed to enhance the health and productivity of submerged soils, promoting ecosystem sustainability and resilience in the face of environmental change.

With gratitude and anticipation

Anandkumar Naorem

Contents

Preface..................... *v*

Submerged Soils 1
Kind of Soils 1
Soil Compaction and Pudding 4
Water Retention and Brans Mission..................... 4
Soil Temperature 5
Long-term Effects 6
Wet Season..................... 7
Dry Season..................... 7
Transformation's of Nutrients (Nitrogen) 13
Iron 17
Fundamentals of Soil Physics 20
Gas Movement and Exchange 24
Convective Flow of Air in Soil 24
Gas Content and Composition 27
Composition of Soil Air 28
Measurement of Soil Air Content and Composition..................... 29
Diffusion Process 31
Soil Temperature and Heat Glow..................... 35
Hydrodynamic Dispersion 44
Combined Transport of Solute 45
Energy States of Soil Water 47
Total Soil Water Pot 48
Classical Thermodynamic..................... 50
Soil Moisture Characteristic Curve..................... 59
Long term Experiments..................... 61

Interrelation IPS of Principal Factors Affecting Soil Quality 63
Submerged Soils 70
Measurement of Soil Moisture Potential 79
Measurement of Soil-Moisture Charac Curve 82
Water Flow in Saturated Soil 84
Darcy's Law 80
Water Flow in Unsaturated Soil 101
Slowly Permeable Black soil 110
Effect of Modification of Soil Phy. Root Growth 111
Crop Yield and Input use Eff. 111

– Submerged Soils –

- saturated with water – sufficiently long time in a year – distinctive gley horizons – due to oxd-red processes :–
  - i) partially oxidized A horizon → ↑ in OM
  - ii) mottled zone → oxd-red alternate
  - iii) permanently reduced zone → bluish green.

- Kinds of sub-soil
  - i) continuous – static 2.5-7.5 cm depth (generally 15 cm depth or more – same potential to produce yield similar to 2.5 cm)
  - ii) alternate

- Importance
- Rice – only major food crop – grown under various degrees of subm.
- charac of sub-soils :–
  - a) greater amt. of soil soln
  - b) reduced O_2 level
  - c) reduced aerobic microbial activity
  - d) an altered chemical status
- systems of rice cultivation
  - semi-dry – rice as rainfed crop esp. uplands. – yield low.
  - wet system ↓ lowlands – irrigation available yield high.

- Properties of Subm. soils

Physical Prop.

i) Diffusion of molecular O_2 and development of aerobic anaerobic layer:

- soil → submerged → water replaces air in pore spaces – except thin layer at soil surface and layer below plough sole soil layers → virtually O_2 free – few hours after subm.
- O_2 diffusion in water layer above soil → slow
- rate of O_2 consumption is high in reduced soil.

- O_2 trapped - blocked pore spaces - utilized by facultative anaerobic organisms.
- more O_2 consumption > available supply → results - formatn of two distinct layers: -

a) oxidized/aerobic surface layer - O_2 present
b) reduced/anaerobic layer - no free O_2

- Thickness of aerobic layer = $\frac{O_2 \text{ supply from atm.}}{O_2 \text{ consump. in soil}}$; $\frac{\text{supply}}{\text{demand}}$

- O_2 reaching subm. soil utilized as: -

✓ a) electron acceptor by soil m/o → cell respiration
✓ b) chemical oxd of Fe^{2+} and Mn^{2+}
✓ c) biological oxd - NH_4^+-N → NO_3^--N
S^{2-} and S^0 → SO_4^{2-}

- If demand > supply → thin oxidised layer
- soil rich in OM → thin oxidised layer

ii) Aeration status of a subm. soil

- gaseous exchange restricted
- magnitude of this effect - evident from relative values of diffusion coeff. in air and water

$$V = -aD(T/T_a)^2 \cdot \frac{dp}{dl}$$

V = Volume of gas, 0.C $cm^2 sec^{-1}$
a = porosity factor
dp/dl = pressure gradient
T = absolute temp.

For O_2 → $\frac{D_{water}}{D_{air}} = 10^{-4}$ and change of po 'a' and dp/dl → insignificant compared with diffusion coeff - so. entry of O_2 and other atm gases - restricted

- net result → low O_2 concent.
  CO_2 ↑ esp. when conditions – favourable – bio activ

iii) Accum of CO_2

- CO_2 and CH_4 accumulate — may escape as bubbles — when pressure builds up.
- 1st week of subm → CO_2 concn ↑ 2.5 t ha^{-1}
- large amt. of carbonic acid (H_2CO_3) → affects chemical equilibrium in soil water system containing Ca^{2+}, Mg^{2+}, Fe^{2+}, Mn^{2+}
  ↓
  pCO_2 will determine solubility of these cations.

- chemical equilibria:–

$$pH = K - \frac{2}{3} \log pCO_2$$

- pCO_2 in reduced soil – determine pH, Eh, solubility of cations
  thereby affects ← specific conductance
  – cation exchange reacns

- ↑ pCO_2 → due to accm of CO_2 initially ← aerobic respiration
  ↓ f.b
  so, pCO_2 in soils ↑ D.M is ↑ ← anaerobic decomp of OM

- higher pCO_2 in acid soils than neutral: — due to ↑ proportion of H_2CO_3.

$$\frac{(H_2CO_3)}{(HCO_3^-)} = \frac{(H^+)}{K}$$

- But ↓ pCO_2 after 1-2 week after subm:—
  a) escape from soil.
  b) diluting effect of CH_4 – produced – later period of OM decomp.
  c) reduction of CO_2
  leaching losses and removal of CO_2 as insoluble carbonates

↓ rapid of CO_2 in soils high in Fe and Mn:—

$$Fe^{2+} + CO_3^{2-} \rightarrow FeCO_3$$
$$Mn^{2+} + CO_3^{2-} \rightarrow MnCO_3$$

(v) Soil compaction and Puddling

Soil compaction:

↳ rearrangement of soil solids → compression of liquid and gaseous phase → volume change → ↑ density

↳ affects H_2O retention, H_2O intake rates and gaseous exc.

↳ BD, microvoids, thermal cond and diffusivity, nutrient mobility ↑

↳ macrovoids, HC and water intake rates ↓

↳ medium texture → more suscep. to compaction

↳ dry pulverized soil → can't be compacted to high density – due to incompressible nature of soil part and high internal friction.

↓

as moist. cont. ↑ → thickness of water films around soil particles ↑ → cohesion among part ↓ → compacted readily

(BD) – when soil compacted → all voids filled with H_2O – no soil H_2O expelled → soil saturated → BD maximum.

$$\rho_B = \frac{\rho_p \, \gamma_w}{1 + \frac{\rho_p w}{100}}$$

(ρ_B – BD; ρ_p – PD; γ_w – unit wt of H_2O; w – water content)

(Water retention and transmission)

↳ affected both as change – pore size distribution – fabric geometry

– compacted soils → less H_2O retain at low suction and saturation

but ↑ H_2O retain at high suction

So, – compaction ↑ plant avai. H_2O.

(Gaseous exch.)

↳ primarily a function of air-filled pore or aeration porosity.

↳ destroyed with compacta → limits gas transfer

(Soil temp)

↳ determine energetics of soil-plant interactions

↳ compaction - modify fabric geometry, soil-H_2O relations

→ Thermal cond of soil particles > air → increased density

↓ volume of gases and ↑ thermal contact between soil part.

T.D ↑
T.C ↑

– Thermal diffusivity = $\frac{\text{Thermal cond.}}{\text{vol. heat capacity}}$ = ↑ as T.C ↑

Thermal con. ↑

heat flow ↑

– So, T.D ↑ as comp and saturation ↑.

So, soil compaction → ↓ percolation losses and ↓ water reqd. of rice → practical and economical tillage practices than puddling for increasing rice yield and WUE.

Puddling

– breakdown soil aggregates at near saturation → into ultimate soil particles.

– ↓ apparent specific vol. of soil

– soils > 20% clay – prone to puddling.

Influence of puddling on soil prop

Short term effects

i) Soil structure :– destroys aggreg and peds – wetting dry soil – uneven swelling aggre – explosion of trapped air – agg. slaked. neither structurally nor chemically uniform puddled layer.

ii) BD and soil strength :– depends on soil aggregation before puddling – If puddling produces – parallel, closely packed structure from well-agg. open structure → BD ↑.

If more open structure → BD ↓.

Puddling ↓ shear strength of surface layer. Shear strength ↓ with MC ↑ and ↑ with ↑ in BD.

iii) Soil porosity:

- individual clay part - parallel rows within water-saturated capillary pores.
- effect depends on soil particle orientation
- If more open structure - total porosity ↑.

iv) Gas exchange

- severely restrict - O_2 exchange
- CO_2 concn ↑

v) Water retention and movement

↳ exceeds than that of unpuddled

- Puddled soils - dry more slowly - because higher unsaturated HC of puddled soil - keep surface soil wet during evaporation - by supplying H_2O from lower layers.

Long-term effects

① - Subsurface hardpans - due to physical compaction and ppt of Fe, Mn and Si

- Cemented pans - generally - in oxidised subsoil - 15 cm - 20 cm deep by ppt of Fe, Mn, Si from upper reduced soil layers.
- But continuous submer - excessively reduced cond - Fe, Mn pans form very slowly.

② Ferrolysis - lower soil productivity

- clay decomposition and tranformation under influence of periodic redn of iron oxides to Fe^{2+}.
- some operate in wet season (reduced cond)

some dry season (oxidised cond)

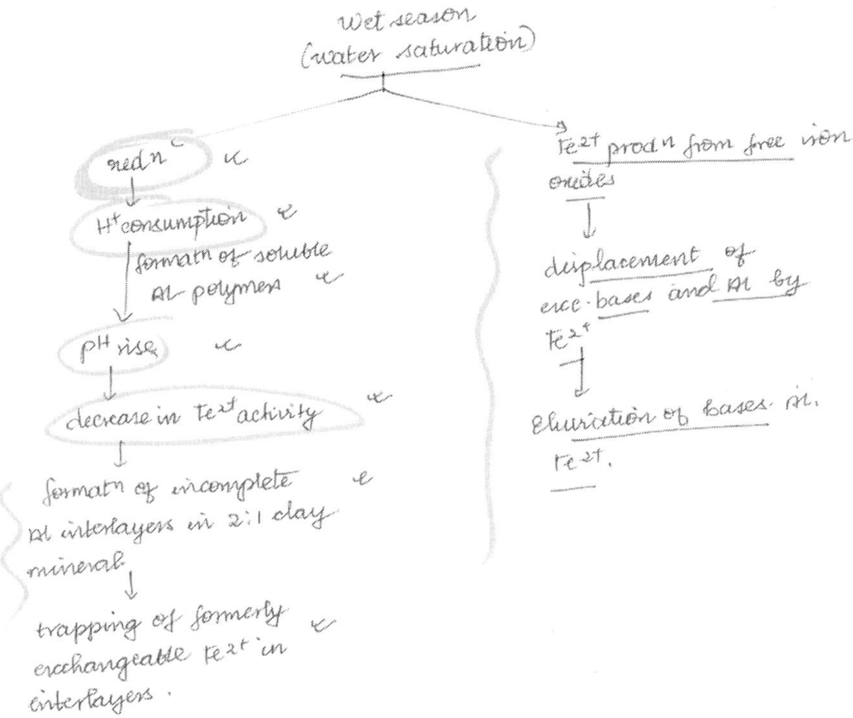
Wet season
(water saturation)
redn
H+ consumption
formatn of soluble
Al polymers
pH rise
decrease in Fe2+ activity
formatn of incomplete
Al interlayers in 2:1 clay
mineral
trapping of formerly
exchangeable Fe2+ in
interlayers.
Fe2+ prodn from free iron
oxides
displacement of
exc. bases and Al by
Fe2+
Eluviation of bases. Al.
Fe2+.

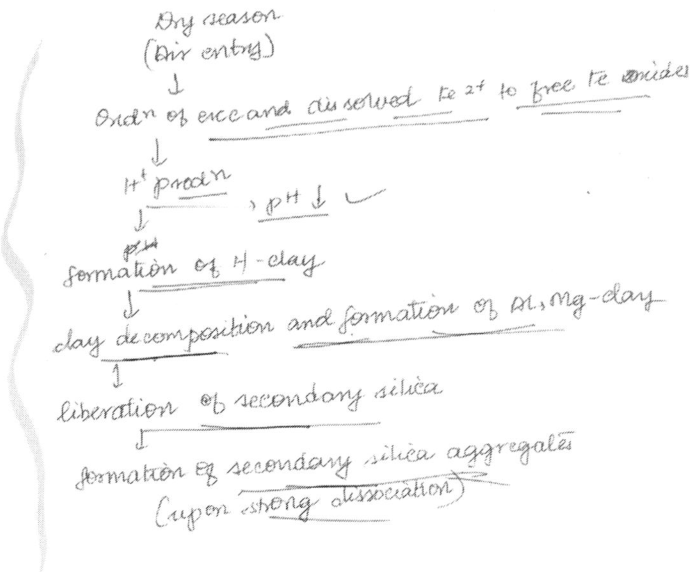
Dry season
(Air entry)
Oxdn of exc and dissolved Fe2+ to free Fe oxides
H+ prodn
, pH ↓
formation of H-clay
clay decomposition and formation of Al, Mg-clay
liberation of secondary silica
formation of secondary silica aggregates
(upon strong dissociation)

- not desirable for rice crop growth
- can be stopped by :-

i) eliminating oxd. phase
ii) eliminating redn phase - rapid leaching - great loss of N and other nutrients or by shifting to upland rice.
iii) raising dry season (oxidised) pH by liming
iv) replacing basic cation lost - fertilizing / liming / base rich water irrigation

- partially effective (i) since clay decomposition - rapid in first few days after air entry and (ii) resupply and even distribn of bases - slower process.

Electro-chemical changes

- main changes :-

i) ↓ in redox pot (Eh)
ii) ↑ in pH of acid soil and ↓ in pH of alkaline soils.
iii) ↑ in specific cond.
iv) cation exchange reactions involving Fe^{2+} and
v) sorption and desorption of ions.

Redox potential

- sequential form
- oxd-reduction → gains e^-
  ↳ losses e^- and ↑ oxidation no
- driving force of chemical reacn - free energy of the system to decrease - until at equilm - sum of free energies of products = reactants

change in free energy ΔG

$Ox + ne \rightleftharpoons Red$

$$\Delta G = \Delta G^0 + RT \ln \frac{(Red)}{(Oxd)}$$

~~which~~ free energy change when activities are unity

converting from calories → volt

$$\Delta G = -\eta EF$$

$$E = E_0 + \frac{RT}{\eta F} \ln \frac{(Oxd)}{(Red)}$$

voltage of 2 reaction

$$E_h = E_0 + \frac{RT}{\eta F} \ln \frac{(Oxd)}{(Red)}$$

↳ when E measured against standard hydrogen electrode

- Eh — quantitative measure - tendency - given system - to oxidise or reduce
- Eh = +ve and high → strongly oxid.
- Eh = −ve and low → ,, red.
- no neutral point as in pH
- When aerobic soil subm → sharp drop in Eh → within few days → −ve as −300 to −400 mV depending presence of OM, Fe and Mn content, pH and temp and bac. potentials.
- Soil reduction per se is not harmful for growth of rice — unless — too low Eh — sulphide formation
- Under rice cultivation, three conditions:—

a) upland - highly oxidised condition → NH_4^+-N → NO_3^--N → leach or denitrify.
- oxd. of organic residues → liberate CO_2, NO_3^-, SO_4 etc.
- availa. of Fe, Mn, P → limited — as in oxidised form
- pH too low → Al toxicity.

b) Healthy reduced state
- NH_4-N - large and - absorbed on soil colloids → very little leaching and deni. losses — 7
- avail. of Fe ↑ due to redn of Fe^{3+} → Fe^{2+}

- H_2S not form generally
- If formed, ppt as insoluble FeS.

$$Fe^{3+} + e^- \rightleftharpoons Fe^{2+}$$

$$Fe^{2+} + H_2S \longrightarrow FeS \downarrow$$

(iron sulphide)

- pH = 6.5 = optimum for avail. of all macro and micro nutrients.

iii) Highly reduced toxic state

- iron toxicity Fe, S^{2-}, as
- Sulphide (S^{2-}) ions accm - toxicity to rice roots
- generation of organic a, ethylene, mercaptans, organic sulphides — harmful.

- how Eh influences rice growth —

a) ↓ Eh — germinatn and seedling emergence
 - but no harm to growth of well establish plant

b) destroys NO_3-N - favours NH_4^+-N accm — increase in soil nitrogen regime
 N fixation → net increase in soil nitrogen regime

c) ↑ availabi. of N, P, Fe, Si, Mn, Mo

d) ↓ " " S, Cu, Zn.

Sequential redn

- after O_2 disappear - need for e^- acceptors by facult. and obligate anaerobes - redn of several oxidised soil comp.

→

ONMF CSC H3

gamed

Redox pot (Eh), mV

$O_2 + 4H^+ + 4e \rightleftharpoons 2H_2 \longrightarrow +830$ gmd ↑

$NO_3^- + H_2O + 2e^- \rightleftharpoons NO_2^- + 2OH^- \rightarrow +430$ rmd +ve

$MnO_2 + 4H^+ + 2e^- \rightleftharpoons Mn^{2+} + 2H_2O \rightarrow +410$ gild

$Fe(OH)_3 + e^- \rightleftharpoons Fe^{2+} + 3OH^- \rightarrow +130$ lmd

Pyruvic a $CH_3COCOOH + 2H^+ + 2e^- \rightleftharpoons CH_3CHOH + COOH \rightarrow -180$ lgd (-ve)

$SO_4^{2-} + H_2O + 2e^- \rightleftharpoons SO_3^{2-} + 2OH^- \rightarrow -490$ rqd

$CO_2 + 2H + 2e^- \rightleftharpoons HCOOH \rightarrow -620$ bond

$H_3PO_4 + 2H^+ + 2e^- \rightleftharpoons H_3PO_3 + H_2O \rightarrow -700$ todd

$H_3PO_3 + 2H^+ + 2e^- \rightleftharpoons H_3PO_2 + H_2O \rightarrow -920$ qnd

$H_3PO_2 + H^+ + e^- \rightleftharpoons P + 2H_2O \rightarrow -930$ qmd

Critical redox potential values

mV

$O_2 \rightarrow H_2O \longrightarrow +380$ to $+320$

$NO_3^- \rightarrow N_2$, $Mn^{4+} \rightarrow Mn^{2+} \longrightarrow +280$ to $+220$

Fe^{3+} to $Fe^{2+} \longrightarrow +180$ to $+150$

SO_4^{2-} to $S^{2-} \longrightarrow -120$ to -180

$CO_2 \longrightarrow CH_4^+ \longrightarrow -200$ to -280

pE concept

↳ for study of redox equilibria

↳ neg. log. of electron activ.

$$pE = -\log(e) = \frac{Eh}{2.303\ \frac{RT}{F}} = Eh/0.0591 \text{ at } 25^\circ C.$$

$$pE = \frac{Eh}{2.303\ \frac{RT}{F}} = \frac{Eh}{0.0591} \text{ at } 25^\circ C$$

Soil pH

- pH ↓ min^m then ↑ asymptotically → stable value of 6.7 – 7.2.
- overall effect : ↑ pH of acid soil (except low in Fe)
  ↓ pH of alk. soil.
  makes pH converge to neutral pH.
- ↑ pH → acid → due to :—
  a) red^n of Fe^{3+}, Mn^{4+}
  b) presence of OM enhance soil red^n.
- soil red^n → H^+ consumption → pH rises.
- ↓ pH in alkaline/calcareous — due to
  ↑ conc. of CO_2 released - decomp. of OM
  ↓
  produces H^+ ions reacting with soil H_2O → ↓ pH

$$OM \xrightarrow{decom} CO_2 \xrightarrow{H_2O} H_2CO_3 \xrightarrow{Dissocia.} H^+ + HCO_3^-$$

- pH of submerged alkali / subm. calcareous } → governed by $Na_2CO_3 - H_2O - CO_2$ / $CaCO_3 - H_2O - CO_2$
- Soils ↑ in OM and reducible Fe → attain pH 6.5 – within few weeks.
- But soils ↓ OM and active Fe — slowly attain pH < 6.5
- Acid SO_4^{2-} soils → low in Fe — may not attain pH of more than 5 even after months —
- OM magnifies ↓ in pH of sodic and cal. soil.
- Low temp or NO_3^- presence retards ↑ pH

- soils ↑ in OM and active Fe^{2+}
- Low temp and NO_3^-

Specific cond

→ ↑ → max^m → declines → fairly stable value — varies with nature and prop. of soil.

→ ↑ → due to release of Fe^{2+} and Mn^{2+} from insoluble Fe^{3+}, Mn^{4+} oxide hydrates

→ accm of NH_4^+, HCO_3^- and $RCOO^-$

→ in calcareous soils — dissoln of $CaCO_3$, $MgCO_3$ by CO_2 and org $\bar{a}$

→ ↑ concn of Ca, Mg — due to displacement of ions from soil colloids

$$Ca^{2+}\boxed{clay} + Fe^{2+} \rightleftharpoons Fe^{2+}\boxed{clay} + Ca^{2+}$$

$$\downarrow\uparrow$$

$$Fe_3O_4 \cdot nH_2O \ (ppt)$$

→ ↓ → ppt of Fe^{2+} as $Fe_3O_4 \cdot nH_2O$

Mn^{2+} as $MnCO_3$

→ cal. soil — fall in pCO_2 and decomp. of org. acids.

→ kinetics of SC — varies widely — soil prop.

strongly acid laterite → ↑ steep SC — first week.

Soils ↑ OM → higher peaks.

cal. soil low in OM — no marked change in SC.

CHEMICAL TRANSFORMATIONS OF NUTRIENTS

[NITROGEN]

— aerated oxidised

$$\text{Organic } N_2 \xrightarrow[\text{ammonif.}]{\text{mineral.}} NH_3^+ \xrightarrow{\text{microbial oxd}} NO_2^- \xrightarrow{\text{microbial oxd}} NO_3^-$$

— anaerobic — absence of O_2 → restrict Nitrosomonas activity

$$\text{Org. } N_2 \xrightarrow{\text{minerali}} NH_4^+.$$

— accm of NH_4^+ → good index → meet up demand of N.

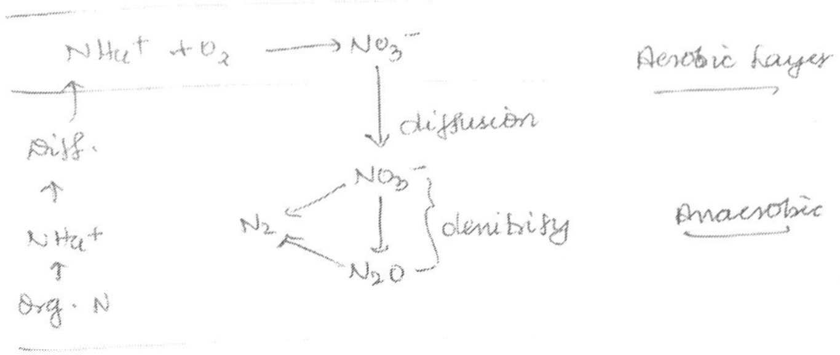

— gradient

→

[Phosphorus]

- P → not directly involved in oxd-red reacn
- but because of its reactivity with the redox elements
  behaviour significantly affected by waterlogging
- P chemistry linked with Fe
- In aerobic soil: P chemically associated with Fe —
  a) Insoluble Iron Phosphate compd – strengite
     $FePO_4 \cdot 2H_2O$
  b) more soluble phosphate compd — Ca and Mg phosphates
     that are co-ppt with insoluble ferric oxyhydroxides.

→ submergence → concn ↑ and then ↓.
↓
magnitude depends on soil prop.

→ ↑ in P avail: — reasons: —

a) Release of P — mineraln of organic residues
b) Redn of $FePO_4 \cdot 2H_2O$ → $Fe_3(PO_4)_2 \cdot 8H_2O$
   ↑ solubility of $FePO_4 \cdot 2H_2O$ and $AlPO_4 \cdot 2H_2O$ caused by
   ↑ pH → redn of acid soil.

c) Release of co-ppt or occluded P — red^n of ferric oxyhydroxides
d) Displacement of P from ferric & Al Phosphates by org. anions.
e) ↑ solubility of Ca phosphates caused by ↓ pH → ↑ CO_2 in calcareous soil.
f) anion exchange → clay and phosphate or org. anion with P.

→ decrease :- ~~reas~~ reasons:-
a) fixat^n (adsorption) - clay colloids (kaolinite, mont, hyd. oxides of Fe and Al)
b) ↓ solubility of P asso. with Ca

→ Max^m phosphate solubilit → under low pH conditions.
→ So, more P → released to soln from soil under submerged cond than upland.
→ Alternate wett and dry → ↓ avail of P in Al-P fraction
→ ↑ ~~av~~. Fe-P fraction.

[POTASSIUM]

- regulated by
Intensity and quantity factor
- soluble K ⇌ Exch. K ⇌ non-exc. K ⟷ mineral K.
- with subm ⟶ Fe^{2+} and Mn^{2+} ↑ ⟶ displaces K^+ in soln ⟶
→ release of K^+ from micas depends on —

a) tetrahedral rotation
b) degree of tetra. tilting
c) -OH group orientation
d) degree of K^+ depletion from soln
e) H_3O^+ ion
f) biolog. activity
g) complexing org. acids, inorg. cations.

non-exc. form. in subm.

- avail. of applied K ↓ in submerged soil - formation of sparingly soluble Fe-K complex.

[SULPHUR]

- red^n of SO_4^{2-} to sulphide (S^{2-})
- dissimilation of amino ā, cysteine, cystine and methionine to H_2S
- Methylthiol found - subm.
- bad odour of putrefying Bg bacteria — due to dimethyl sulphide and methyl, butyl and isobutyl thiols.
- main product is H_2S.
- Fe^{3+} red^n preceeds SO_4^{2-} red^n.
- So, Fe^{2+} reacts with H_2S to form insoluble FeS.
- protects m/o and plants from toxicity
- But if low in Fe - muck and sandy (peat) soil — Fe inactivated by complex formtn with OM — H_2S toxicity possible.
- In subm — SO_4^{2-} ↑ and then ↓.
- ↑ due to release of SO_4^{2-} from strongly sorbed clay and hydrous oxides of Fe and Al at low pH.
- Rice takes up SO_4^{2-}. red^n of SO_4^{2-} → S^{2-} reduces SO_4^{2-} avail.
- But oxidised at root zone
- So, three implications:—
  a) insufficient sulphur supply
  b) Zn and Cu immobili.
  c) H_2S toxicity (soils low in Fe).

[IRON]

- most important chemical change
- red^n of Fe^{3+} and ↑ in its solubility.
- factors:-
  time of subm, amt of om, active Fe, active Mn, nitrate etc
- due to red^n → soil colour → brown → gray
- Fe^{2+} conc^n ↑ then ↓ slowly

→ ↑ due to red^n

$$Fe(OH)_3 + e^- \rightleftharpoons Fe^{2+} + 3OH^-$$
(insoluble) (soluble)

→ ↓ due to ppt of Fe^{2+} as $FeCO_3$ in early stages where pCO_2 high and as $Fe_3(OH)_8$ when ↓ in pCO_2

$$2Fe^{2+} + 3CO_2^{+} \rightarrow 2FeCO_3$$
(insoluble)

- Rice - benefits → ↑ in Fe but suffer in acid soils - excess
- consequences:
  i) conc^n of water soluble Fe increases.
  ii) pH ↑.
  iii) cations displaced from exchange sites
  iv) solubility of P and Si ↑
  v) new minerals formed.

[Mn]

- red^n of $Mn^{4+} \rightarrow Mn^{2+}$
- almost similar to Fe trans. - because Mn tran. governed by redox equilibria system.
- ↑ water soluble Mn^{2+}, ppt of $MnCO_3$ and reoxd^n of Mn^{2+} diffusing to oxygenated interfaces.
- in aerobic laterite soil - subm - red^n of Mn^{4+} concurrently with NO_3^- red^n → but this red^n preceeds Fe red^n.

→ water soluble Mn^{2+} ↑ then ↓

redn ← → ppt as $MnCO_3$, $Mn(OH)_2$

→ redn → range +200 to +400 mV

→ OM influences transf :–

i) prodn of complexing agents → ↓ activity of free ~~Fe~~ Mn in soln

ii) ↓ in oxd-red pot of soil directly/ind. through microbial acti.

iii) stimulation of microbial ac. → results in corp. of Mn in biological tissue.

Course no ACSS-655

— Monitoring Physical, chemical and Biological changes in soils – long term fertilizer experiments (LTFE)

- Long term: approx to reality. no artefacts
- exp. conducted on same set of exp. sites over a sequence of years
- Preplanned sequence of treatments or crops or both to quantify small changes in properties over time.
- some have ~~been~~ to be modified
  eg. Rothamsted exp – same variety can't be used now which was used before long time.

- > 20 years
- Importance
- born to study organic manure to increase crop yield (agronomic)
- judge decline in yield after many years (sustainability)
- law of diminishing return
- budgeting nutrient
- ~~eg.~~ Indo Gangetic Plains → P build up due to appli. since last 40 years so, can advise not to use P now ~~bcz~~. need not ~~experiment~~
  (framing emperical rules)
- ~~we can profess with~~ we can give prophecy supported by the observation from the exp.

- crop rotation
  eg. Rice - rice, rice - wheat
  If rice - rice has more yield but at the cost of Global warming,
  we must advocate rice - wheat
- Residual effect of nutrient
- Only master/primary treatments are considered because of expensive nature – well thought, planned.
- Tillage exp – not that old in India
- Irrigation schedules – based on LTFE → C.R.I. for wheat
- Cropping system – sustainable but cheap.

Fundamentals of Soil Physics

— Hillel

Soil water: content and potential

- Neutron scattering
- neutron moisture meter — 2 components
  - probe — lowered into an access tube inserted vertically into soil — contains source of fast neut and detector of slow neut
  - scaler/ratemeter → monitor the flux of slow neutrons scattered by the soil.
- source of fast neutron → by mixing radioactive emitter of alpha particles (helium nuclei) with Be.
  → 2.5 millicurie pelletized mixture of Ra and Be. → common.
- Ra-Be source emits 16,000 neutrons/sec/mg of Ra (mcurie)
  → energy vary from 1–15 MeV (milli electron volts) (mainly 2-4 MeV)
  → speed 1600 km/sec. — so fast neutrons.
- alternative to fast neutrons → mixture of Am and Be
- Both Americium and Ra — emit γ-radiation but Am — lower energy (so less hazardous)
- source material — chosen — based on longevity
  → Ra-Be — ½ life 1620yr — so they are choosen —
- fast neutrons → omitted radially soil → collide elastically with atomic nuclei → By repeated collision — neutrons deflected, scattered — lose some kinetic energy
  → approaches a speed — characteristics for particles at ambient temp. — correspond to 2.7 km/sec with energy – 0.03 eV
- → said to be thermalized
  → slow neutrons
  → continue to interact with soil
  → eventually absorbed by nuclei present

- effectiveness of various nuclei present in soil in thermalizing fast neutrons varies widely

↓

avg loss of energy is maximal for collisions between particles of same mass.

↓

So, of all nuclei in soil – ones most nearly equal in mass to neutrons – are hydrogen nuclei – so, most effective fast neutron moderators of all soil constituents.

- avg no. of collisions – to slow down a neutron

H – 18
C – 114
O – 150

9N+6 – for larger mass no N.

- If soil contains appreciable ~~amt~~ concn of H – thermalized fast before they get far from source → slow neutron scatter randomly in soil – form a swarm/cloud of constant density around probe.

↓

- determined by – rate of emission by source
  - rate of thermalization
  - absorption by soil.

- But some elements (B, Cd, Cl) – of non-negligible concentration – decrease density of slow neutrons.

- Generally, density $\propto$ nearly concn of H in soil and so more or less $\propto$ volume fraction of water present

i.e. $N_w = m\theta + b$ — count rate in water/standard absorber

and $N_w/N_s = y\theta$ — vol wetness.

slow neutron count rate in wet soil

m, b = slope
x = Intercept

- slow neutrons – detector cell – filled with BF_3 gas.

↓

If encounters ^{10}B nucleus – and absorbed – α particle emitted – creating an electrical pulse on a charged wire.

↓

no. of pulses over measured time interval – counted by scaler or indicated by ratemeter.

PROBE
↓
DETECTOR
↓
SCALER.

- sphere of influence – effective volume of measurement.

radius – ≤ 10 cm – wet soil
≥ 25 cm – dry soil.

↳ so, disadvantages
makes it unsuitable for detection of moisture profile discontinuities (eg. wetting fronts or boundaries between distinct layers)

+ surface soil measurement – precluded

↓

due to escape of fast neutrons through surface.

But advantage:– relatively large volume monitored – advantage in H_2O balance studies – as such volume – more representative of field soil than much smaller samples taken for gravimetric

- Another disadv – assumed – neutron thermalization in soil due solely to the presence of water. – But in actual situation appreciable amounts of H – clay and OM.

+ Boron – content in soil – lower slow neutron density
↳ also for Cl.

↓

If B concn > 10 ppm
Cl conc > 1000 ppm } affect calibration curve

- safety issues - radiation - neither seen nor felt -
- Advant: easy and fast.

GAS MOVEMENT AND EXCHANGE

- Two main processes:-

Convection

↓

Mass flow

moving force:- gradient of total gas pressure – cause in entire mass of air to stream from a zone of higher pressure to lower pressure zone.

Diffusion

↓

moving force: gradient of partial pressure (concn) of any constituent member of – variable gas mixture —

causes molecules of unevenly disturbed constituen to migrate from a zone of higher concentration to lower – even gas as a whole – isobaric and stationary

CONVECTIVE FLOW OF AIR IN SOIL

- what induces convective flow?
  - pressure diff. between soil air & outside atm.
  - barometric pressure changes.
  - temp. gradients
  - wind gusts
  - penetration of water during infiltration
  - fluctuation of shallow water table pushing air ↑ or ↓
  - extractn of soil water by plant roots
  - during tillage or compaction by machinery (– short term)
- Mostly diffusion considered – more important.
- But, – convection → at shallow depths and in soils with large pores
- mostly similar to that flow of H_2O.

  ↳ flow of both air & H_2O impelled by and is ∝ to — pressure gradien

- dissimilarity ② – relative incompressibility of water in comparison with (air)

  ↓

  highly compressible

  Density and viscosity strongly dependent on pressure (as well as temp)

(ii) gravitational pot. (in case of vertical flow) — cause water to flow but hardly involved in air flow.

(iii) H_2O — greater affinity to surfaces — mineral particles drawn into narrow necks forms capillary films and wedges (menisci)

— Air tends to occupy larger pores. but coexist with H_2O

— in soil occupying different positions

Reason why soil exhibits towards two fluids different conductivity or permeability functions — as they relate to — different effective diameters, tortuosities and interconnectedness of the pore.

— we can formulate convective flow of air in an eqn analogous to Darcy's law for water flow: —

$$q_v = -(k/\eta)\nabla P$$

k → permeability of air filled pore space

q_v → volume convective flux of air (volume flowing through unit cross sectional area per unit time)

η = viscosity of soil air

∇P = 3-dimensional gradient of soil air pressure.

→ One dimension

$$q_v = -(k/\eta)\frac{dP}{dx}$$

If flux express — mass per unit area & per unit time

$$q_m = -(\rho k/\eta)\frac{dP}{dx}$$

q_m → mass convective flux

ρ = density of soil air.

— We know that,

ρ depends on pressure and temperature,

assuming soil air — ideal gas in which

$PV = nRT$.

$PV = nRT$ — no. of moles of gas; T — absolute temp.; R — universal gas constant per mole; P — Pressure; V — Volume

Since $\rho = \frac{M}{V}$ — mass M = no. of moles 'n' times molecular wt 'm'.

$M = n \cdot m \Rightarrow n = \frac{M}{m}$

$\Rightarrow PV = \frac{M}{m} RT$

$\rho = (m/RT) P$

From continuity equation for a compressible fluid...

$$\frac{d\rho}{dt} = -\frac{dq_m}{dx}.$$

$Pm = \frac{M}{V} RT$

$\Rightarrow Pm = \rho RT$

$\Rightarrow \rho = \left(\frac{m}{RT}\right) P$

Substituting ρ

$$(m/RT)(dP/dt) = \frac{d}{dx}\left[\left(\rho k/\eta\right)\frac{dP}{dx}\right]$$

If $\rho k/\eta$ nearly constant (if pressure diff. are small)

$$\frac{dP}{dt} = \alpha \frac{d^2P}{dx^2}$$

where $\alpha = \frac{RTk}{m}$. = composite constant

→ approximate eqn for transient state convective flow of air in soil.

→ assumption: flow is laminar

- But diff. mechanism of convective movement → transfer of dissolved gases by rain or irrigation water infiltrating into and percolating through soils.

- O_2 saturated air at atm. pressure contains 6 litres of O_2/m^3 → only enough to provide for respiration of 1 kg (dry wt) of active roots —

$$\frac{d\rho}{dt} = -\frac{dq_m}{dx} \rightarrow$$

$$\Rightarrow \frac{d\left(\frac{m}{RT}\right)P}{dt} = \frac{d}{dx}\left[\left(\rho k/\eta\right)\frac{dP}{dx}\right]$$

$$\Rightarrow \frac{m}{RT}\frac{dP}{dt} = \frac{d}{dx}\left[\left(\rho k/\eta\right)\frac{dP}{dx}\right]$$

If $\rho k/\eta$ = constant, $\rho = 1, \eta = 1$

$$\Rightarrow \frac{m}{RT}\frac{dP}{dt} = \frac{d}{dx}\left[k \frac{dP}{dx}\right]$$

$$\Rightarrow \frac{dP}{dt} = \frac{RTk}{m} \cdot \frac{d^2P}{dx^2}$$

$$\Rightarrow \frac{dP}{dt} = \alpha \cdot \frac{d^2P}{dx^2}$$

— GAS CONTENT AND COMPOSITION —

- respiration - plant roots absorb O_2 and release CO_2
- except in rice - O_2 supply / internal transfer from above-ground parts to roots - not sufficient - of the roots
- Gas moves in — air phase (rate of transfer of gases in air phase) generally higher than — water phase

so, soil aeration depends largely on volume fraction of air filled pores.

Volume fraction of soil air

- volume ratios of three constituent phases - solid, water and air → continually changing as soil undergoes wetting and drying, swelling and shrinkage, tillage, compaction, aggregation etc.
- Since water and air → pore spaces — their vol. frac. related — ~~or~~ an increase of one → decreases of another ↑ → ↓

$f_a = f - \theta$ — volume frac. of H_2O (volume wetness)

f_a — vol. fra. of air; f — Total porosity (fractional vol. of soil not occupied by solid)

air filled porosity

↓

since f_a → dependent on soil water content — f_a used as an index of soil aeration ~~in cor~~ + some wetness value

↓

field capacity.

so volume fraction of water retained by a freely draining soil profile after the initially rapid stage of internal drainage.

or

field air capacity :- Fractional volume of air in soil at f.c water content.

- Air capacity — depends on — soil texture.
  - In sandy soils → 25% or more
  - Loamy soils — 15 - 20 %
  - Clayey soils — < 10% of total soil volume

– Soil texture and soil structure imp
↓
well aggregated – more macropores
↓
so, air capacity → 20–30%

– But when clay dispersed – block the pores
↓
air capacity may < 5%.

– Limitations of using air capacity as index for soil aeration

(a)
– difficult – determine value – accurately
↳ since it depends on prior determination of two highly variable parameters – cumbersome to measure
↓
f.c and total porosity
both depend on method of sampling
– results grossly inaccurate

(b)
rate of exchange of soil air rather than simply the content of soil air constitutes decisive factor

↳ at high wetness values — occluded air — form a part of air filled volume – don't contribute to active gas exchange.

and thin surface crust → limit aeration – regardless of air filled porosity beneath.

Composition of soil air

– comp. of soil air – close to open atmosphere
↳ Reason: – oxygen consumed in soil – readily replaced from atm and CO_2 readily vented into atm.

– greater diff — concn of CO_2 – reason: aerobic respiration by roots – higher plants + macro-organisms + microorganisms.

CO_2 in ~~soil~~ atmosphere: 0.036% – 360 ppm in terms of partial volume.
↓
soil: 10 times or more

- Because CO_2 produced – soil – by oxd^n of carbonaceous matter (om)

↓

↑ in CO_2 concn → asso. with ↓ O_2 concn

but not necessarily to an exactly commensurate degree

Since additional sources – O_2 – dissolved form and in easily reducible compounds.

Eg. If O_2 conc^n of air is > 20% — 100 fold increase of CO_2 in soil can diminish O_2 concn only to about 17 %.

Measurement of Soil air content and composition

- earlier – determine air filled porosity – at std. value of soil wetness.

↳ done by – undisturbed sample ↳ – at field capacity assumed

↓

Practically, sampling in field 2 days after a deep wetting or saturating in laboratory – then subjected to tension

uncertainties

↓

no real indication of aeration dynamics.

— gas chromatograph technique using syringe —

Measurement – soil respiration

- field respirometers.
- Respiratory quotient = $\frac{\text{vol. of } CO_2 \text{ produced}}{\text{vol. of } O_2 \text{ consumed}}$

Diffusion of gases in the soil

diffusivity of O_2
in $H_2O \rightarrow 2.6 \times 10^{-5}$ cm²/sec
air $\rightarrow$ 0.226 cm²/sec

- diffusive transport of gases — occurs partly in gaseous and partly liquid phase.
- those occurs through air filled pores – maintain exc. of gases between atm and soil
- those – water films — maintains supply of O_2 as to and disposal of CO_2 from live tissues
- For both pathways — Fick's Law

$$J_g = -D\left(\frac{dc}{dx}\right)$$

J_g — diffusive flux of a gas; dc — mass concn (mass of diff. sub / vol); dx — distance; D — Diff. coeff (dimension of area per time)

dc/dx = concn gradient

If partial pressure 'p' instead of concn

$$J_g = \left(-\frac{D}{\beta}\right)(dp/dx)$$

β — ratio of $\frac{P}{C}$ (P — partial pressure, C — concn)

- For diffusive path in air phase

$$D_S < D_0$$

D_S — diffusion coeff in soil; D_0 — bulk air

Reason:- limited fraction of total volume occupied by continuous air filled pores and due to tortuous nature of these pores

So, $D_S \rightarrow$ function of f_a – air filled porosity.

Penman (1940)

$$\frac{D_S}{D_0} = 0.66 f_a$$

0.66 — Tortuosity coeff — apparent (straight line) path is 2/3rd length of mean path of diffusion in soil.

- But, tortuosity – depends on fractional vol. of air filled pores.

Reason :– Tortuous path length should increase as the air filled pore volume decreases.

So, Penman — limited range of f_a or of θ

- de Vries (1950) — relation between effection Diff. coeff and f_a → curvilinear – depends on pore geometry

Diffusion process

For transient conditions — continuity principle.

$$\frac{dc}{dt} = -\frac{dJ_g}{dx}$$

↓ Time rate of change of concn of a diffusing gas = rate of change of diffusive flux with distance.

assumption :- diffusing substance - conserved - neither created nor destroyed within the soil body.

$$\frac{dc}{dt} = -\frac{dJ_g}{dx} \pm S(x,t)$$

$S(x,t)$: To take account of amount of diff. sub. added to or substracted from system per unit time

source, sink term ↓ function of both space and time.

+ = increment rate (source)

– = decrement rate (sink)

considering only vertical direction z :–

$$\frac{dc}{dt} = \frac{d(D_s\, dc/dz)}{dz} \pm s(z,t)$$

If D_s = constant.

$$\frac{dc}{dt} = D_s\,(d^2c/dx^2) \pm s(z,t)$$

In aggregated soils – diffusion between macropores — drained rapidly after a rain / irrigation — form continuous air filled phase.

However within aggregate micropores ← remain nearly saturated for extended periods — restrict internal aeration of agg.

so, plant roots - often confined to larger pores between agg.

Assuming an agg. isotropic and approx. spherical

$$\frac{dc}{dt} = \left(\frac{1}{r^2}\right) \frac{d\left[D_s r^2 \left(\frac{dc}{dr}\right)\right]}{dr} \pm S$$

radial dist. from centre of sphere.

- Diffusion of O_2 to roots — Lemon (1962)

divided process — 2 regions

Inner region (root itself) — i

Outer (water film enveloping root) — e

- For steady state diffusion,

$$D_i\left(\frac{d^2c_i}{dr^2} + \frac{1}{r} + \frac{d^2c_i}{dr}\right) - S = 0$$

$$D_e\left(\frac{d^2c_e}{dr^2} + \frac{1}{r} + \frac{d^2c_e}{dr}\right) = 0$$

If D_i (diff. coeff for root) and D_e (water film) are known and O_2 consumption rate per length of root S known — possible to solve — define the conditions likely to limit root resp. for different conditions

- Fundamental diff. between relation of soil's permeability to pore geometry and to diffusion coeffs.

Permeability pertains to pressure induced viscous flow — obeys Poiseuille's law — flow rate varies with 4th power of pore radius. — So permeability — strongly dependent upon pore size distribution.

But,

Diffusion — depends on total volume and tortuosity of continuous pores available for diffusion.

why diff. not dependent on pore size distri? — for air at atm. pressure, the mean free path of molecules in thermal motion is of order of 0.0001 - 0.0005 mm — much smaller than radii of pores → that generally accounts for most of soil's fa.

But exception — diff. of gases in porous medium under extremely low gas pressure — phenomenon - Knudsen diffusion

↓

occurs when mean free path of gas molecules >> than pore radius

Measurement of Convection and diffusion

- To characterize soil aeration — air permeability

↓

coeff. governing convective transmission of air through soil in response to a gradient of total gas pressure.

Techniques

↓

- constant pressure
- falling pressure devices.

applied in field and used in assessing openness of surface layer to entry of air as affected by such cultural practices as tractor traffic or tillage.

- measurement of diffusion rates through air filled pores alone — no indication of possible impedance of liquid envelope surrounding root

↳ A soil - ↑ O_2 concn in large pores that are open to atm but no adequate supply to roots if thickly hydrated roots.

- Another method - for measuring O_2 diffusion to a rootlike probe — based on use of thin platinum elect. - maintained at constant potential.

→ -ve charge electrode → dissolved O_2 mol. reaching root by diffusion - takes up 4 e^- and react with H ion — form H_2O in an acid soln

$O_2 + 4H^+ + 4e^- \rightarrow 2H_2O$ or

react with H_2O → hydroxyl in an alkaline soln

$O_2 + 2H_2O + 4e^- \rightarrow 4OH^-$

↓

resulting current measures flux of O_2 to moisture covered electrode (which acts as sink) — simulating the action of a respiring root.

Practically

↳ Insert probe into a moist soil

↓

wait until reading steady

↓

time the flux of O_2 to probe — represent O_2 supplying power of the soil — ODR (Oxygen diffusion rate)

↓

But not in dry soils

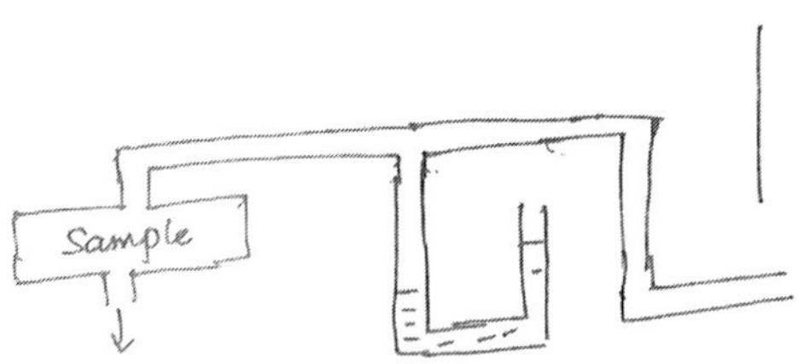

Soil temperature and heat flow

Modes of energy transfer

- radiation, convection and conduction

↓

emission of energy in the form of electromagnetic waves from all bodies above 0K.

Acc. to Stefan-Boltzmann Law – total energy emitted by a body, J_t integrated over all wavelengths $\propto$ absolute temp, T^4 of body's surface

$$J_t = \varepsilon \sigma T^4$$

σ – constant

ε – emissivity coeff = 1 for perfect emitter (generally black body)

T also determines wavelength distrib. of emitted energy.

Wien's Law

wavelength of maximal radiation intensity, $\lambda m \propto \frac{1}{T(\text{abs. Temp})}$

$$\lambda_m = \frac{2900}{T}$$

λ_m – µm

Planck's Law

Radiative intensity as a function of wavel and temp

$$E_\lambda = \frac{C_1}{\lambda^5 [\exp(C_2/\lambda T) - 1]}$$

C_1 – constant; C_2 – constant

E_λ – energy flux emitted at a given wavelength

- Since soil surface temp — 300 K — radiation emitted by soil surface has its peak intensity – at wav. of 10 µm and wav. dist over range 3-50 µm. — in realm of infrared/heat radiation

- Sun - acts as black body - effective surf. temp - 6000K

↓

radiation — visible light range — 0.3 - 0.7 μm

— infrared (greater wav) — upto 3 μm

— uv radiation — < 0.3 μm

little overlap between these spectra - customary to distinguish

↓

incoming solar radiation - short wave rad.

spectrum emitted by earth - long wave rad.

Convection

- movement of a heat carrying mass.

Conduction

- propagation of heat within a body - by internal molecular motion

↓

Because temp - expression of K.E of a body's molecules - existence of temp - indicates transfer of K.E by collisions of rapidly moving molecules from warmer region to their neighbours in colder region.

↓

So, analogous to diffusion.

- Fourth composite mode:- Latent heat transfer

↓

eg. distillation - includes heat absorbing stage of evaporation, f.b convective/ diffusive movement of vapour and ending with heat releasing stage of condensation.

Conduction of heat in soil

- 1822 – Fourier – mathematically analogous to Fick's law (diffusion eqn) as well as Ohm's Law for conduction of electricity and Darcy's law for water flow in soil.

- First Law of heat conduction

Fourier's Law

flux of heat in a homogeneous body – is in direction of and proportional to temp gradient

$$q_h = -\kappa \nabla T$$

κ – kappa (Greek) – thermal conductivity

∇T – spatial gradient of temp. T.

q_h – Thermal flux (amt of heat conducted across a unit cross-sect. area in unit time)

One dimensional

$$q_h = -K_x \frac{dT}{dx} \quad \text{or} \quad q_h = -k_z \frac{dT}{dz}$$

$\frac{dT}{dx}$ – temp gradient in any direction

k_z – for non-isotropic

$\frac{dT}{dz}$ → specially vertically ⊥ represents soil depth ($z = 0$ being soil surf)

–ve sign:- heat flows from higher temp to lower (in the direction of, and in proportion to, a –ve temp gradient)

$q_h = -\kappa \nabla T$ = sufficient under steady state conditions
- temp at each point in conducting medium is invariant
- flux constant in time and space

- Second Law of heat conduction

Principle of energy conservation in form of continuity eqn:—

In absence of internal sources or sinks of heat — time rate of change - heat content of a volume element must = change of flux with distance

$$\rho c_m \left(\frac{dT}{dt}\right) = -\nabla q_h$$

'C' ↓ specific heat capacity per unit volume

ρ — mass density

c_m — specific heat capacity per unit mass ↓ Change in heat content of a unit mass of the body per unit change in temp.

∇q_h ↳ 3-dimensional gradient

$\frac{dT}{dt}$ = time rate of temp. change

ρ = total mass per unit volume — includes H_2O in moist soil.

$$\rho c_m \left(\frac{dT}{dt}\right) = -\left(\frac{dq_x}{dx} + \frac{dq_y}{dy} + \frac{dq_z}{dz}\right)$$

x, y, z = orthogonal direction co-ordinates

So, second law: —

$$\rho c_m \left(\frac{dT}{dt}\right) = -\nabla (K \nabla T)$$

One dimension

$$\rho c_m \left(\frac{dT}{dt}\right) = \frac{d}{dx}\left[K\left(\frac{dT}{dx}\right)\right]$$

↓ same $\pm S(x,t)$ ↓ sources and sinks of heat

Thermal diffusivity, D_T

$$D_T = \frac{K}{C}$$ — K = thermal conductivity; C = volumetric heat capacity

$$D_T = \frac{-q_h/\left(\frac{dT}{dx}\right)}{C}$$

$\Rightarrow$ ~~$q_h = D_T$~~

$$\Rightarrow D_T C = \frac{-q_h}{dT/dx}$$

$$\Rightarrow q_h = -D_T C\,(dT/dx) \Rightarrow q_h = -\alpha C_v\left(\frac{dT}{dx}\right)$$

Thermal properties of soil

↳ vol. heat capacity C.

↳ Thermal conductivity K

↳ Thermal diff. D_T

Vol. heat capacity

change ~~of~~ a unit's volume heat content per unit change in temp

↳ cal/cm³/K or J/m³/K

So, C – depends on comp. of soil solid phase, BD, soil wetness

$$C = \Sigma\left(f_{si}C_{si} + f_w C_w + f_a C_a\right)$$

f = ~~vol.~~ vol. fraction of each phase (solid – ~~s~~ si)
(water – w)
(air – a)

avg. C = 0.48 cal/cm³ K (0.rag)
or 2.0×10^6 J/m³ K. } mineral composing soil.

= 0.6 cal/cm³ K
2.5×10^6 J/m³ K } org.

Thermal cond and diff.

- Thermal cond = quantity of heat transferred through a unit area of conducting body in unit time under a temp gradient
  - depends on mineral comp and OM content + vol. fraction of H_2O and air.
- ✓ Since K of air << water/solid → ↑ air content correspond to ↓ K
- ✓ K is also time variable (since proportion of H_2O & air vary continuously)
- ✓ K influenced by depth (soil comp. vary depth)
- ✓ K = temp.
- ✓ Unlike C → K sensitive not only to mineral comp.
  - but also sizes, shapes, arrangement — soil part.

In normal soil wetness range —

C undergo 3 fold or 4 fold change

but k — 100 fold or more

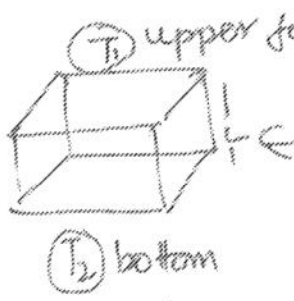

← constant heat flux, q_h passing ∝ temp grad. (temp gradient) with k_c as prop. const

$$q_h = -k_c\left(\frac{dT}{dx}\right) = -k_c\frac{(T_2 - T_1)}{L}$$

Since cube mixture of two phases — composite

k_c will be intermediate betwn k_0 and k_1

Acc. to Vries (1975)

$$k_c = \frac{f_0 k_0 + k f_1 k_1}{f_0 + k f_1}$$

k = ratio of avg temp gradient in particles / corresponding gradient in continuous fluid

$$k = \frac{(dT/dz)_2}{(dT/dz)_1}$$

for unsaturated soil →

$$K_c = \frac{f_w k_w + k_s f_s k_s + k_a f_a k_a}{f_w + k_s f_s + k_a f_a}$$

k_w, k_a and k_s = specific thermal conductivities of the soil constituents

k_s = ratio $\frac{\text{space avg. of temp grad. in solid phase}}{\text{water phase}}$

depends on grain shapes as well as mineral, org. comp

Thermal diff. D_h m^2/sec

– change in temp produced in unit vol. by quantity of heat flowing through the volume – unit time – under a unit temp. gradient

– $\frac{\text{conductivity}}{\text{Product of specific heat \& density}} = D_h = K/c_s\rho = K/C_v$

C_v – vol. heat capacity

Convective Transport of solutes

- also called Darcian flow

flux of solutes $J_c \propto$ concn c

$$J_c = qc = -c\left[K\left(\frac{dH}{dx}\right)\right]$$

$$q = -K\left(\frac{dH}{dx}\right)$$

as q = volume of liquid flo. through – unit area – per unit time
c = mass of solute per unit vol. of soln
so, J_c = mass of solute passing – unit cross sectio. area – per unit time

- To estimate distance of travel per unit time, average apparent velocity $\bar{v}$

$$\bar{v} = \frac{q}{\theta}$$ — vol. wetness

gross approximation — taken as straight line length of path traversed per unit time
disregard roundabout path caused by geometric tortuosity of water filled pores.

$$J_c = \bar{v}\theta c$$

- Sometimes – average residence time, t_r of solute within a layer of soil of thickness L

$$t_r = \frac{L}{\bar{v}}$$

speed = $\frac{\text{distance}}{\text{time}}$

If flow – impelled by gravity alone – no pressure gradients then downward flux of liquid = hydraulic cond. K of medium,

$q = K(\theta)$ as K function of θ

$$t_r = \frac{L}{\bar{v}} = \frac{L\theta}{q}$$

$$\Rightarrow t_r = \frac{L\theta}{K(\theta)}$$

Diffusion of solutes

— Occur within multicomponent gaseous / liquid phases in consequence of random thermal motion and repeated collisions and deflections of molecules in fluid.
↳ Brownian motion

— Whenever solutes not distributed uniformly throughout soln
↓
concn gradient exists
↓
solutes tend to diffuse from ↑ concn → ↓ concn

$J_d = -D_0 \left(\frac{dc}{dx}\right)$ — solute's effective concn gradient
↳ diff. coef for a partic. solute diffusing in bulk H_2O

J_d — rate of diffusion
related to Fick's law (first)

— For diffusion in soil's liquid phase:—

effective diff. coeff D_s << diff. coeff in bulk water, D_0

Reason

— Liquid phase — only a fraction of soil volume
only at saturation ⇒ vol. fraction = soil's porosity

— Soil's pore passages — tortuous — actual path >> than apparent str. line

— as soil wetness ↓ → fractional vol. of diffusion in liq. phase ↓ → tortuous length ↑.

If sole factors affecting D_s in soil are fractional water volume θ and tortuosity ξ,

$$D_s = D_0 \theta \xi$$ — tortuosity factor (< 1)

$$\xi = \frac{\text{straight line}}{\text{average roundabout}}$$

So, ξ → depend on both fractional vol. and geometric configuration of H_2O phase.

so, $\downarrow\theta \longrightarrow \downarrow\xi$

D_s ⟶ strongly dependent on θ

So, $D_s(\theta)$

For unsaturated soil. —

$$J_d = -D\left(\frac{dc}{dx}\right)$$

$$\Rightarrow J_d = -D_s(\theta)\left(\frac{dc}{dx}\right)$$ } → steady state diffusion.

For transient → include mass conserv. law ~~are~~ expressed in continuity eqn.

$$\frac{dc}{dt} = -\frac{dJ_c}{dx}$$

$$= -\frac{d}{dx}\left[D_s(\theta)\frac{dc}{dx}\right]$$

when D_s = constant → it forms Fick's second law of diffusion

$$\frac{dc}{dt} = D_s\left(\frac{d^2c}{dx^2}\right)$$

But, D_s is generally not constant — dependent not only on θ but also c → θ and c

Hydrodynamic dispersion

— in inhomogeneous soln in porous body | erratic movement of solute from ↑ concn → ↓ concn

— ~~which predominates over diffusion~~.

. results from microscopic nonuniformity of flow velo. in soil's conducting pores.

— since H_2O moves faster — wide pores and centre of each pores — some portions of flowing soln move ahead while other lag behind

$D_h = a\bar{v}$ — average flow vel.

↓ (from D_h): dispersion coefficient

↘ (from a): empirical parameter

Additive diffusion-dispersion coef (D_{sh})

- function of θ and $\bar{v}$

↓ (θ): fractional water volume

$$D_{sh}(\theta, \bar{v}) = D_s(\theta) + D_h(\bar{v})$$

Combined transport of solutes

J =

combined solute flux = [flux due to convection] + [flux due to diffusion] + [flux due to hydrody. disp]

$$J = \bar{v}\theta c - D_s(\theta)\left(\frac{dc}{dx}\right) + D_h(\bar{v})\frac{dc}{dx}$$

$$J = \bar{v}\theta c - D_{sh}(\theta, \bar{v})\frac{dc}{dx}$$ } steady state (time invariant)

↓ limited to noninteracting (inert) solutes

↓ (inert solutes): no adsorption, no reactions — hardly exist

and D_s, D_h, θ, $\bar{v}$, c — can be defined only in macroscopic terms.

↓ so, approximation eqn.

- Transient - fluxes and concn vary both in time and space — continuity principle.

for combined transport,

$$\frac{d(c\theta)}{dt} = -\frac{dJ}{dx}$$

rate of change of solute mass in a volume element of soil = diff. between incoming and outgoing fluxes of solute

$$\frac{d(c\theta)}{dt} = -\frac{d(v\theta c)}{dx} + \frac{d}{dx}\left[D_{sh}\frac{dc}{dx}\right]$$

For steady → $\theta, \bar{v}, D_{sh}$ → constant

$$\frac{dc}{dt} = -\bar{v}\frac{dc}{dx} + \frac{D_{sh}}{\theta}\frac{d^2c}{dx^2}$$

Certain solutes generated within the soil. eg. NO_3^- ion — evolves under nitrification

$$\frac{d(c\theta)}{dt} = -\frac{dJ}{dx} + S \text{ — source-sink term}$$

$$S = \sum_{i=1}^{n} S_i - \sum_{j=1}^{m} S_j$$

n possible sources

m possible sinks.

Adsorption of ions

adsorption of ions = +ve = attachment of cations to clay surfaces.

= −ve = repulsion or partial exclusion of anions from electrostatic double layer of same clay.

$$[\theta + A(c)]\frac{dc}{dt} = \frac{d}{dz}\left(D_{sh}\frac{dc}{dz}\right) - \frac{d(qc)}{dz} + S$$

$A(c)$: slope of adsor. isotherm — $f(c)$

θ, c, S, q → f(depth, time)

D_{sh} → $f(\theta)$ and $f(\bar{v})$

ENERGY STATES OF SOIL WATER.

- soil water – contain energy – diff. quantities and forms
- classical physics – 2 principal energies

kinetic

↓

$\propto v^2$

- as soil water movement quite slow

↓

kinetic – neglected

potential

↓

due to position or internal condition –

determine state and movement of soil H_2O.

- diff. – in P.E of water between one point and another – tendency – water flow
- higher pot to lower
- obeys same universal pursuit of elusive state (equil^m)
- rate of decrease of P.E with distance → moving force.
- work must be done – from lower pot – higher pot.
- since P.E measure of amt. of work – knowing the P.E. state of water in soil and in plant – helps to estimate how much work plant – must expend to extract H_2O.
- not an absolute amt. of P.E contained in H_2O
- but relative level of P.E in different regions within soil.
- standard reference state – hypothetical reservoir of pure H_2O

↓

at atm. pressure

same temp as that of soil H_2O

at a given and constant elevation.

- energy increment = force × distance increment
- force = $\frac{\text{energy increment}}{\text{dist. incre.}}$
- force = $\frac{\text{P.E incre.}}{\text{dist. incre}}$ → negative pot. gradient

$-\frac{d\phi}{dx}$

→ force acts in direction of decreasing pot

- concept of soil-H_2O pot - replaces arbitary categories.
- Potential concept in soil water — Buckingham (1907)
  Potential dependent on H_2O content — Gardner (1920)
  Tensiometer - measuring pot insitu - Richards (1931)

- when soil-saturated - H_2O at hydrostatic pressure > atm pressure — P.E of that water > P.E reference state — H_2O tend to move spontaneously from soil ⟶ reservoir.

- If soil-moist but unsaturated - water no longer free to flow out toward a reservoir at atm pressure

- In saturated (if no osmotic effect) - Potential = +ve.
- Unsaturated - water constrained by capillary and adsorptive forces = Pot = -ve
- P.E - reduced by presence of solutes.

TOTAL SOIL WATER POT

- Thermodynamically -
  P.E — diff in partial specific free energy - soil water and standard water.

- Soil Physics terminology committee of the Int. Soil Sc. Society
  ↳ total pot. of soil water ⟶ amt. of work done — that must be done - per unit quantity of pure H_2O - in order to transport reversibly and isothermally - an infinitesimal quantity of water - from pool of pure H_2O - at a specified elevation at atm. pressure to soil H_2O (at the point under consideration)

↓

just a formal definition

- In actual practice - potential not measured by transporting H_2O - but by measuring some other property related to potential.

- Infinitesimal quantity → because — to ensure determination procedure doesn't change either ref. state or soil-H_2O pot.
- defn based on specific differential Gibbs free energy function.
- Philip (1960) – integral form of thermodynamic function
- Soil H_2O – subjected to a no. of force fields – which cause pot. diff – from pure water.

↓ results from the
- attraction of the solid matrix for H_2O
- presence of solutes
- action of external gas pressure
- gravitation.

total potential ← (these factors)
↓
sum of separate contributions of these factors:–

$$\phi_t = \phi_g + \phi_p + \phi_o + \ldots$$

- ϕ_g – grav. pot
- ϕ_p – pressure (matric) pot)
- ϕ_o – osmotic pot.
- ... – ellipses – additional terms

[gpo]

- not all of separate pot – act in same way
- their gradients – may not be always equally effective in causing flow – eg osmotic pot. gradient – requires semi-perm. membrane
- main adv:– provides unified measure by which state of H_2O can be evaluated anytime and everywhere within soil plant atmosphere continuum. (SPAC)

THERMODYNAMIC BASIS

- Classical thermodynamics — deals – equilm states and reversible processes – describe forces acting on water and its energy on retention
- But equilm states – rare in nature + spontaneous processes → irreversible.

↓
non equilm or irreversible themodyn. —

classical thermodynamic relation

- soil H_2O pot concept - depends upon - 1st and 2nd laws of classical thermodynamics.
- First law — energy conserv. law — neither created nor destroyed but from one form to another.

$$dQ = dU + PdV + dW$$

| UVW |

- dW → all other work done by sys - on its surro.
- dU → change in internal energy U of the system
- dQ → heat added to system
- PdV → work of expansion done by system (P pressure, V - volume)

- 2nd law - direction of change in an isolated system is always toward equil^m.

↳ stated in different ways.

Mathematically,

second law - rests on defn of 2 properties
- absolute temp T (always +ve)
- entropy S

$dQ = TdS$ (for reversible process)

$dQ < TdS$ (for irre)

- dS → change in entropy.
- dQ → heat input into system

Intensive prop = temp, pressure and concn
↳ independent of size of the system

extensive prop = mass, volume
↳ system as a whole.

entropy - measure of internal disorder or randomness of a system.

$$dQ = TdS$$

$$\Rightarrow dS = \frac{dQ}{T}$$

In irreversible process, $dS > 0$ ⇒ entropy tends to increase spontaneously.

So, 2nd law :–

$$dU = TdS - PdV$$

change in internal energy U of the system

In system of variable composition — total differential of internal energy — function of S, V and n_i ↳ no. of moles of a given component in syst.

$$dU = \left(\frac{dU}{dS}\right)_{V, n_i} dS + \left(\frac{dU}{dV}\right)_{S, n_i} dV + \left(\frac{dU}{dn_i}\right)_{S, V, n_j} dn_i$$

Gibbs free energy $G = U + PV - TS$

chemical pot. μ_i of a component in a system – variable comp = partial molal Gibbs free energy of that component $= \bar{G}_i$

↳ change in free energy of system with change in concn of the component considered =

$$\bar{G}_i = \left(\frac{dG}{dn_i}\right)_{T, P, n_j} = \mu_i$$

Total differential of chemical pot

$$d\mu_i = \left(\frac{d\mu_i}{dT}\right)_{P, n_i} dT - \left(\frac{d\mu_i}{dP}\right)_{T, n_i} dP - \left(\frac{d\mu_i}{dn_i}\right)_{T, P, n_i} dn_i$$

↳ expression of pot. energy state of a component in a mixed system in absence of external forces — when T, P, composition – only effective variables.

↳ excludes gravitational effects. centrifugal or externally imposed electrical force fields.

↳ so, constant in system when intensive parameters – constant and a state of equi^m exists.

- But in unequilibrated system – diff in μ_i between 2 locations determines the direction (not rate) in which component will tend to move spontaneously within the system.

- Limitation/difficulty: ~~for~~ formulation – working equation for potential of soil water → selection of ~~inpedent~~ independent variables so that they don't overlap.
↓
due to complex nature of forces of interaction between H_2O and solid matrix.

- diff. in μ_i between H_2O in soil and pure free water at same temp = moisture pot. of soil.

Gravitational Pot.

- everybody on earth's surface – attracted towards center of earth by gravitational force:—
↳ = wt of the body
↓
product of mass of the body × gravitational acceleration.

- To raise a body against attraction – work must be done – this work stored by the raised body in form of — gravitational P.E.
↳ amount depends on body's position in gravitational force field.

- determined by elevation of the point – relative to some arbitrary reference level.
↳ set at the elevation of a
- for sake of convenience pertinent point within the soil or below soil profile.
↓ so that gravit. pot = +ve always or zero.

- But if soil surface - chosen as reference level (often done) — grav. pot below surface = −ve with respect to that ref. level.

- At ht. 'z' above ref, grav. pot. energy Eg of a mass 'M' of water with volume 'v'

$$E_g = Mgh \quad | \text{Mass} \times \text{acc}^n \times \text{ht} |$$

$$= \rho_w vgh$$

(ρ_w: density of H_2O; g: acc^n due to gravity)

Gravitational potential in terms of pot. energy per unit mass

$$\frac{E_g}{M} = \frac{Mgh}{M} \Rightarrow \phi_g = gh$$

per unit volume

$$\phi_{g,v} = \rho_w gh$$

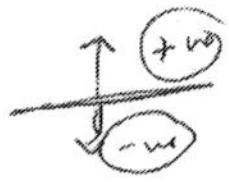

- Grav. pot. — independent of chemical and pressure cond. of soil H_2O
  - dependent only on relative elevation.

Pressure Pot

- When soil water — hydrostatic pressure > atm. pressure → pressure pot = +ve
- When it is at a pressure < atmos. pressure (a subpressure commonly known as tension or suction) ⟹ pr. pot = −ve
- Water under free water surface = +ve Pressure pot.
- " at " " " = 0 Press. pot
- " risen in a capillary tube above that surface = −ve.

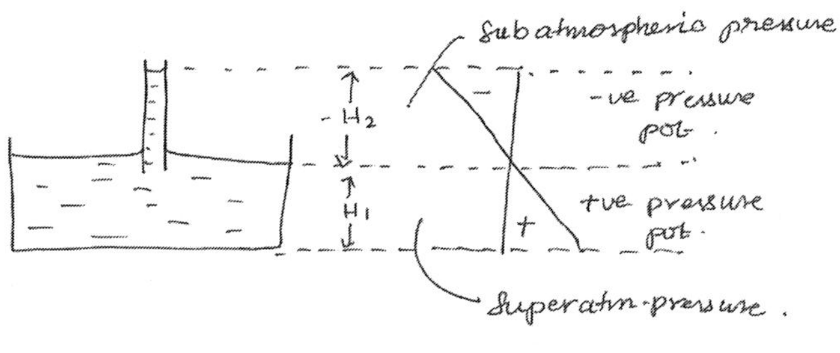

→ +ve press. pot – below ground water level = submergence potential.

→ hydrostatic pressure P of H_2O with reference to atm. pressure

$P = \rho g h$ └ submergence depth below free water surface (known as piezometric head)

Potential energy of this water is then

$\dot{E} = PdV$

and thus submergence pot. taken as pot. energy per unit volume = hydrostatic pressure P

$\phi_{ps} = P$

⇒ –ve press. pot – capillary pot – recently matric pot.

↓ results from capillary and adsorptive forces due to soil matrix.

↓ attract and bind H_2O in soil and lower its pot. energy below that of bulk H_2O.

– capillarity results from

- surface tension of H_2O
- contact angle with the solid particles.

– In unsaturated (3 phase) soil system, curved menisci form which obey the eq^n of capillarity

$$P_0 - P_c = \Delta P = \gamma \left(\frac{1}{R_1} + \frac{1}{R_2}\right)$$

γ – surface tension of H_2O.

P_0 – atm pressure (taken as 0)

P_c – pressure of soil H_2O (< atm pressure)

ΔP – pressure deficit

R_1, R_2 – principal radii of curvature of a point on the meniscus.

– if soils were like simple bundle of capillary tubes, eq^n of capillarity — enough to describe relation between –ve press. pot to radii of soil pores in which menisci are contained.

- In addition to capillary phenomenon, ~~soil~~ → adsorption – forms hydration envelopes over particle surfaces.

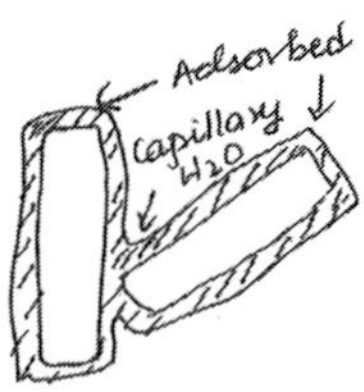

} → two mechanisms of soil-water interaction

- clayey soil – presence of water in films as well as under concave menisci – important
  - ↳ at high suction – influenced by electric double layer – exc. cations

- sandy soils – adsorption – not important
  - ↳ capillary effect predominates.

- Generally, –ve pressure pot — results from combined effect of these two mechanisms
  - ↳ can't be separated since capillary wedges are at ~~equ~~ internal equil^m state with adsorption films. – one can't be changed without affecting other.

- capillary pot – known as matric pot – total effect resulting from – affinity of H_2O – to whole matrix of soil – including pores, particle surface.

- soil water – may exhibit either < –ve ~~pressure~~ matric pot / +ve press. pot } but not simultaneously

- Unsaturated soil – only matric pot (–ve)
  - – no pressure pot or –ve ~~press.~~ ~~pot~~ press. units

- another factor affecting pressure of soil water – possible change in pressure of ambient air.
  - ↳ Generally, this effect – negligible (as atm press. remains nearly constant)

However, in lab – application of air pressure to change soil-water pressure or suction → common practice.

– This effect known as pneumatic pot.

In unsat. soil $\phi_p = \phi_m + \phi_a$

ϕ_m → matric pot; ϕ_a → pneu. pot.

– In absence of solutes – liquid and vapour phase – in unsat porous medium are related at equilm:–

$$\phi_m = RT\ln\left(\frac{P}{P_0}\right)$$

R → gas constant for H_2O vapour; T → absolute temp; $\left(\frac{P}{P_0}\right)$ → relative humidity

P/P_0 = ratio of partial press. of vapour in air phase / in saturation.

Osmotic Pot

– presence of solutes – affects thermodyn. prop. — lowers its potential energy.

– solutes ↓ vapour pressure of soil H_2O.

– it may not affect liquid flow in soil significantly

↓

But it is imp. whenever a membrane or diffusion barrier is present which transmits water more readily than salts.

– osmotic eff – imp in interaction between plant roots and soil. + in processes involv. vapour diffusion.

(Add)

Pressure pot

– To describe swelling and compressible soils –

– Philips (1969) – overburden pot.

↓

where any addn of H_2O to the medium demands a local increase in bulk vol – over. pot – work performed (per unit wt of added H_2O) against gravity and external load

Quantitative exp. of soil-H_2O Pot

- Energy per unit mass
  - fundamental expression
  - ergs/gm
  - J/kg
  - dimensions — L^2T^{-2}
- E. per unit volume
  - water practically incompressible — so. density almost independent of pot.

    direct proportion between expression of pot as energy per unit mass and energy per unit volume.
- per unit volume :- yields dimensions of pressure.

  ↓

  ~~Pre~~ energy = Pressure x volume

  so, $\frac{\text{energy}}{\text{volume}}$ = pressure.

- dynes/cm^2
- N/m^2 (Pa) — ergs/cm^3 — 1 erg = 1 $\frac{\text{dyne}}{\text{cm}}$
- bars/or atm. — 1 bar = 100.0 cm of H_2O head = 10^5 Pa = 100 Jkg^{-1}
- dimension ~~M~~ = $\frac{\text{force}}{\text{area}}$ = $ML^{-1}T^{-2}$
- convenient for osmotic & press. pot. — but hardly for gravit.
- E. per unit wt (hydraulic head)
  - whatever can be expressed in units of hydrostatic pressure — can be exp. in terms of an equivalent head of H_2O — ht of a liquid column corresponding to given pressure.

    ↓

    eg. 1 atm = vertical water column / hydraulic head = 1033 cm

    — for mercury = 76 cm
- simpler and more convenient
- so, potentials → exp in hydraulic head.

Instead of

$$\phi_t = \phi_g + \phi_p$$

$\Rightarrow H = H_g + H_p$ — pressure head.

H — total pot. head of soil water (hydraulic head); H_g — gravit. head

If we use ϕ = potential in terms of energy per mass

P = ,, ,, ,, ,, pressure

H = potential head, then

$$\phi = \frac{P}{\rho_w} \text{ — density of } H_2O$$

$$H = \frac{P}{\rho_w g} = \frac{\phi}{g} \text{ — accn due to gravity.}$$

→ Tension and suction → −ve pressure (subatmos)

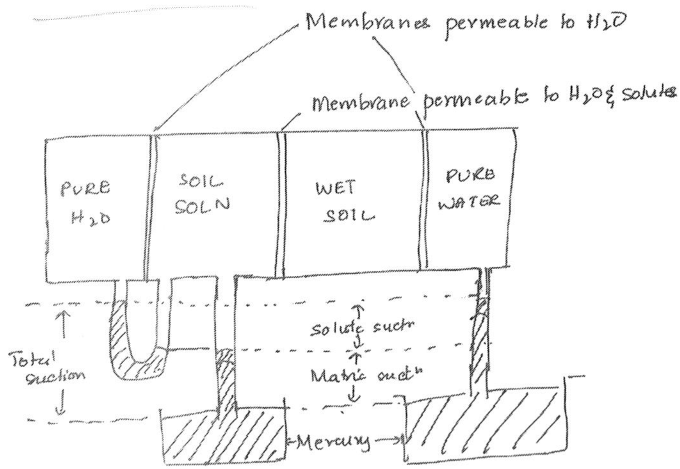

In an isothermal system – equilm — matric suction = pressure diff across membrane (separating soil soln inside from same soln in bulk. ~~between pure water and soln~~.

Osmotic (solute) suction = pressure diff across semipermeable membrane — pure H_2O and soil soln.

Total suction :— sum of matric + osmotic suction

↳ pressure diff across semipermeable — pure H_2O and soil solution.

SOIL MOISTURE CHARACTERISTIC CURVE

– water in sat. soil = atmospheric pressure if at equil^m with free H_2O at same elevation. → 0 hydrostatic pressure
↓
0 suction.

If slight suction (water pressure slightly subatm)
↓
applied to H_2O in sat. soil
↓
no outflow — ~~unti~~
↓
suction increased — critical value — when exceeded → largest pore — begins to empty — water content displaced by air. —
↓
critical suction → (air entry suction) (threshold of desaturation)

Very small for coarse textured soils and well aggregated soils.

Coarse texture ↳ pores are fairly uniform in size ←
↓
~~do~~ distinct critical air-entry phenomenon.
↓
as suction applied → first pores to be emptied are – relatively large ones

Capillary equation $\left(-P = \psi = \frac{2\gamma}{r}\right)$ → gradual ↑ suction → emptying of progressively smaller pores – until high suction – only the very narrow pores retain water.

So, ↑ suction → ↓ thickness of hydration envelopes on soil particle surfaces.

↑ suction → ↓ soil wetness.

- Amt of water remaining in soil - at equilm — function of sizes and volume - of water filled pores and of the amount of H_2O adsorbed to particles

↓

so, function of matric suction

↓

measured experimentally

↓

represented graphically

↓

Curve - soil moisture retention curve or soil moisture release ,, " " characteristic.

- till date, no universally applicable theory - exists for prediction of matric suction vs wetness relationship from basic soil prop.

↓

- adsorption and pore geometry effects — too complex to be described by simple model.

- empirical eqn — describing SMC - for some soils - within limited suction ranges.

Visser (1966)

$$\psi = \frac{a(f-\theta)^b}{\theta^c}$$

ψ — matric suction; f — porosity; θ — vol. wetness

a, b, c = constants

a: 0-3; b: 0-10

$f = 0.4 - 0.6$

- limitation: difficult to evaluate its constants

Long Term experiments

- monitoring physical, chemical and biological changes in soils.
- experiments conducted on same set -exp sites- over sequence of years.
- Preplanned sequence of treatments/crops or both – to quantify small changes – in properties – over time.
- Why LTFE?
  - ↳ to study effect of continuous application of organic/inorganic or both sources — on soil health, crop productivity etc in multiple cropping systems.
  - ↳ assess sustainability of agricultural systems.
  - ↳ nutrient efficiency of different fertilization systems – through nutrient balances.
  - ↳ useful for – framing empirical rules for practical agri.
  - ↳ monitor change in soil prop. in terms of soil ~~quality~~ fertility.

- Importance
- effect of crop rotations on crop yields, soil health and chemical, physical and bio. soil prop.
- eff. of management practices – on nut. dynamics and ecological soil functions.
- interrelations betwn land use systems and envn.
- effect of climatic changes on soil prop.
- indirect quantif. of atmospheric N/S deposition.
- evidence of nutrient efficiency of diff. fertilizn system – through nutrient balances.

- Residue of nutrients → get increase
  ↳ fertilizer recommendation and nut. budget

Traditional Short term exp.	Long term fert exp.
- simple, short term aspect	- broad & long term
- time duration - short	- more
- statistically more sound	- widely assumption based combination of competent planning and transfer of techn.
- considers quantitative aspects mainly	- both
- totally dependent on climate and other envn factors	- less coincide with climate and other envn.
- focus only on initial trajectories.	

Types (fitce)
- fert. exp
- tillage exp
- irrigation
- cropping system
- ecological

JB Sir John Bennet Lawes

JH Sir Joseph Henry Gilbert

- Lawes and Gilbert → a LTFE between 1843 – 1856 (South East England)

main obj:- measure effects of inorganic compounds on crop yields

History

- 1843 : called as Permanent Manurial Exp, Rothamstead, England.
- India – Kanpur (1885) 9 gas
  Pusa (1908) 9doq Imp. of OM, GM on soil prod.
  Coimbatore (1909) 9doq
- 1935 : Shahjahanpur – effect of NPK on soil fert. (9mos)
- 1933 : Padegaon – effect of groundnut cake – on soil fert.

9mon

- WB (Chinsurah and Suri), MP (Indore) and Maharashtra (Sholapur and Pune) : effect of cattle manure / AS on soil fert.
- present - 600 LTE - worldwide - of 720 years.
- India: AICRP - LTFE - standard ref. in Indian cond.
- 18 in India launched in Sep 1970 - ICAR

Ludhiana (Punjab)
Pantnagar (Uttarkhand)
IARI (New Delhi)
Barrackpore (WB)
Bhubaneshwar (Orissa)
Ranchi (Jharkhand)
Raipur (Chattisgarh)
Akola and (Maharash)
Parbhani (")
Bangalore (Karnataka)
Pattambi (Kerala)
~~Jagtial~~
Jagitial (AP)
Coimbatore (TN)
Junagarh (Gujarat)
Udaipur (Rajasthan)
Jabalpur (MP)
Palampur (Himachal Pradesh)

- INTERRELATIONSHIPS OF PRINCIPAL FACTORS AFFECTING SOIL QUALITY.

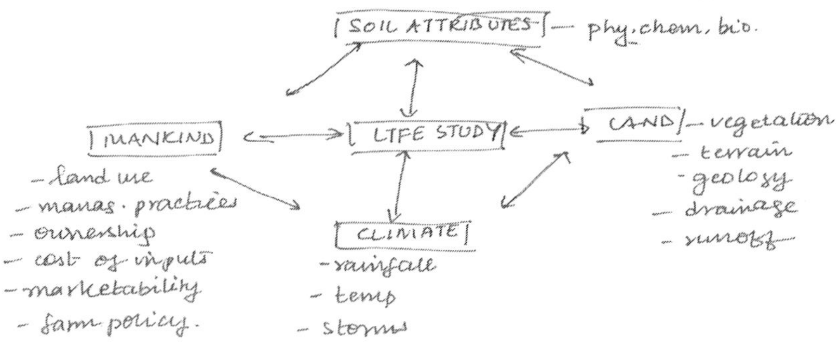

PHYSICAL PROP

→ ↓BD - concomitant ↑ in porosity
↳ more appreciable in NPK+FYM treatments than control and fallow

- ↑HC and MWD - due to continuous growing of crop with fert.
- conjunctive use of fert + om → better
- RDF + FYM → ↑ Macropores especially

PHYSICO- CHEMICAL

→ pH : continuous-fert → ↓ soil pH
↳ Incorp. of FYM+fert – maintain soil pH

→ EC : ↑slight → salt content
↳ due to continuous-fert
↓
don't cause any adverse effect on soil health.

→ CEC : maintain/↑ OC status so → ↑ CEC.

→ ↓ in SOC with ↑depth.

→ ↑ in BD with ↑ depth

→ TOC → RDF+FYM > RDF + PS > RDF + GM > RDF > Control.

→ BD → ~~RDF~~ Control > RDF > RDF +GM > RDF +PS > RDF +FYM

→ depletion of SOC %
NW India > Deccan > NE India > SE India > west coast > E India.

→ SOC sequestration rate (kg ha^{-1} yr^{-1}) → highest
100% NPK+FYM.

→ crop C input - highest
f-b rhizodeposition C
root biomass C.

- During 36 yrs of cropping - left over C is highest in organic amendment as compared to OA + crop resi.
- left over C ~~C applied through CR~~ → OA. OA > CK + OA
- FYM has less C:N ratio than PS ~~and GM~~.

But GM lesser C:N ratio than FYM.

Cellulose content ↑ in PS > FYM > GM

Lignin content ↑ — FYM > PS > GM.

Total C:— PS > GM > FYM.

TILLAGE

- reduced tillages improves SOC in plough layer (15-30 cm)
- Organic amendments fatilitate conversion of crop residue C — to SOC
- more conversion of CR-C to SOC under rice than non-rice facilitated by OA ↓ due to root / straw

To increase SOM status

↳ NPK+FYM
↳ Balanced use of chemical nutrients
↳ Intensive cropping
↳ Suitable crop rotation — Soybean - wheat
↳ GM/Legume crop > Cereal crop.

Decline

- Imbalanced use of chemical nut.
- low addn of manure

Cultivation of soil + use of chemical fert ↑ oxdn of OM ↓ SOM status.

Effect of LTFE on SOC

- decline in SOC - due to imbalance application of chemical fert.
- Fert + FYM maintain ↑SOC over fert only.
- notion 'appln of fert and cult of soil ~~no~~ ↓SOC' → fallacy (misleading notion)

CHEMICAL PROP

- balanced use → ↑ in avail. N. irrespective of cropping systems and soil types
- cropping system with legume → ↑ build up avail. N
- ↑ rainfall and porosity - adversely affect - avail N.
- continuous intensive cropping ↓ Total N and avail N stat

Fertilization & N status ↑ ↓

- FYM + NPK / OM ↑ N status
  - ↳ optimum microbial pop.
  - ↳ Quick mineralization
  - ↳ Restore soil fert.

→ use of organic manure → ↑ P.
→ absence of K in fert. schedule → ↓ avail K.
- use of NPK + FYM ↑ avail K.

↑ soil P status ↓

due to appln of NPK and P fert.

continuous app of N alone (greater removal of P for growth)

In case of pH:— NPK + OA. (neutral)

BD — lowest — NPK+OA

Av. N, P, K — highest – NPK > NPK + OM.

Secondary and micro nut

- use of FYM ↑
  but fert ↓ → exc. Ca, Mg in soils.
- Avail. S content ↓ – intensive crop. esp. when S free fert.
- fert cont. S + FYM ↑ S status
- $ZnSO_4$ @ 25 kg ha^{-1} ↑ avail Zn soil.

BIOLOGICAL PROPERTIES

- ↓ pop. of actinomyc, bac, azotobacter → with ↑ fert use
- Incorp of FYM ↑ popn
- C residues improved soil health — by ↑ micro. pop.
- NPK + FYM ↑ micro. respiration and enzyme act.
- 100% NPK + FYM + lime ↑ SMBC and MBN in soil.
- NPK + FYM ↑ enzyme activity – acid phosphatase
  alkaline phosp.
  phosphodiesterase
- Sustainability yield index (SYI) of all crops — > in NPK + FYM/Lime
- NPK + lime / FYM → for sustain produc.
- FYM – amelioration
  – rule out hidden hunger
- Lime – amendment
  – creates conducive envn in root zone — facilitate plant root growth & avail. of nutrients by contro. soil pH

= ecosystem services considered in long term sites :—

Food – Livelihood – Soil – Fuel – Aesthetics – Water – GHGs – Habitat – Diversity (Nat. hazard. Spiritual enrichm. cognitive developme. Pest Protect.)

- proposed relationship between long term sites (LT sites) and process studies (fundamental research)

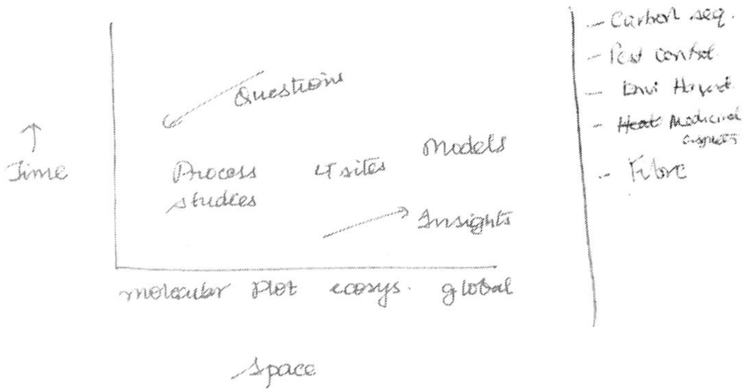

— Limitations

- Chances of spatial variability (S)
- variations in plot size — result edge effect (P)
- Difficult quantifn of landscape scale process. (L)
- no special strategy to get rid on burgeoning envn issues (B)
- problem in inconsistency regarding management and data collection (I)
- direct inf. on economic or social factors that contribute to sustainability is unpredictable (E)
- limited interpretation of time series data on meteorology, crop protection, economic and other soil variable factors change. (T)
- failed to capture range of farmers' practice (F)
- no satisfactory use to generate policy and management recommendation (M)

- not suitable for small scale farming (F)
- cost expensive (C)

Pre-requisites

- larger plots especially for ease of management
- good specific maintainance —
  - a) avoid soil movement
  - b) use suitable gradient
  - c) plough to turn the soil one year in one direction and another year in opp. direction.
- good monitoring over time (recording data)
- need envn. concern
- maintain continuity and integrity of exp.

LTFE

Past view

- not stat. sound (lack of appropriate design with replication)
- no introduction of HYV.
- no application of eff. fert
- mainly mono cropping based
- lack of proper maintainance
- lack of proper orientation
- " " technology

Present View

- sound?
- efficient use of high analysis fert.
- integrated approach
- intensive cropping with suitable strategies
- approach of multiple cropping.

PIE
F^2M
TC
BLS

Submerged Soils

[Contd.]

Zinc

- transf. of Zn – not involved in oxd-red process like Fe, Mn
- But redⁿ of hydrous oxides of Fe, Mn
  - changes in soil pH
  - pCO_2
  - formation - insol. sulphide comp

  ] – influence solubility of Zn either favourably or adversely

- (Favour) solub. of Zn
  - a) redⁿ of hydrous oxides of Fe and Mn
  - b) formation of organic complexing agents
  - c) ↓ pH of alkaline and calcareous soils.
- (Lower)
  - a) formation of hydroxides, carbonates, sulphides
  - c) ~~↑pH~~ combined effect of ↑pH, HCO_3^- and S_2^- formation.
- solub. of native forms of Zn in soils – highly pH dependent
- ~~pH~~ ↓ factor of 10^2 for each unit ↑ in soil pH

(solub.) ↑pH → solubility ↓ (10^2)

- Zn-pH relationship:–

$$Soil + Zn^{2+} \rightleftharpoons Soil - Zn + 2H^+$$

pK value = 6.0 – equⁿ holds good for submerged soil.

- when ~~nativ~~ aerobic soil – submerged – availa. of native as well applied Zn ↓ → magnitude depends on soil prop.
- Transf – depends on depth of submergence and appⁿ of OM.
- Acid soil – submerged – pH ↑ → avail. Zn ↓
- Alkali soil – " – pH ↓ → solub. Zn ↑

Reason - why Zn ↓ due to submergence:

i) insoluble franklinite ($ZnFe_2O_4$) compound

$$Zn^{2+} + 2Fe^{2+} + 4H_2O \rightleftharpoons ZnFe_2O_4$$

ii) very insoluble compds of Zn as ZnS — under intense reducing con.

$$Zn^{2+} + S^{2-} \rightleftharpoons ZnS \text{ (Sphalerite)}$$

iii) insoluble compds as $ZnCO_3$ - at later period - subm - owing to high pCO_2 + due to decomp. of OM

$$Zn^{2+} + CO_2 \rightleftharpoons ZnCO_3 \text{ (Smithsonite)}$$

iv) $Zn(OH)_2$ at relatively high pH — decreases avail. of Zn —

$$Zn^{2+} + 2HO^- \rightleftharpoons Zn(OH)_2 \text{ (Insoluble)}$$

v) Adsorption - soluble Zn^{2+} — by oxide minerals eg. sesquioxides, carbonates, soil OM, clay minerals.

<u>Possible mechanisms for oxide minerals</u>

i)

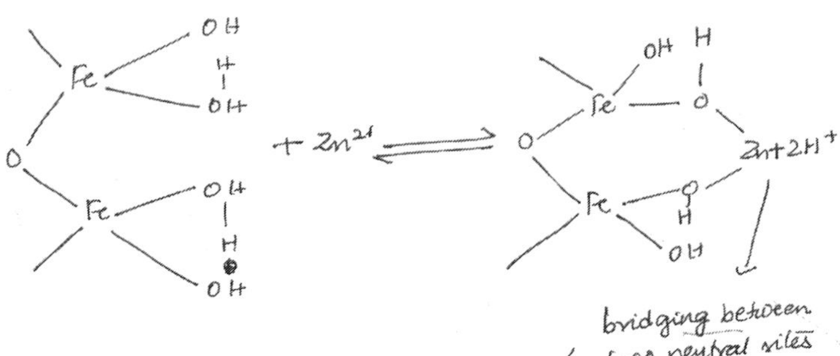

* Zn can also be adsorbed to two positive sites or to a +ve and neutral site

Mechanism II

$$\text{Fe or Al}\begin{matrix} -OH \\ -OH_2 \end{matrix} + \begin{matrix} ZnCl^- \\ \text{or} \\ Zn^{2+} + Cl^- \end{matrix} \underset{}{\overset{\text{low pH}}{\rightleftharpoons}} \text{Fe or Al}-\overset{H}{\underset{OH_2}{O}}-ZnCl + H^+$$

- occurs at low pH
- non-specific adsorption.
- Zn^{2+} is retained – unavailable to plants

vi) other insoluble Zn compounds. eg. high phosphatic fert.

$$Zn^{2+} + PO_4^{3-} \longrightarrow Zn_3(PO_4)_2$$
[Insoluble]

- ZnS (Zn sulphide sphalerite) – in presence of traces of H_2S – control Zn solubility.
- Zn stable – submerged soils.
- ↑ pH and poorer aeration → ↑ Zn deficiency if soil solⁿ Zn activity is controlled by ZnS.
- ↑ Mn → ↓ Zn adsorption.
- Ca, Mg → affect Zn uptake
- Submerged alkali/calcareous soil – high amt of HCO_3^- ions – Zn^{2+} unavailable – $ZnCO_3$ compd.
- avail. of Zn in sub. soil – governed by mutual interaction of quantity (q) and intensity (c) and kinetic parameters as regulated by adsorption, desorption, chelation and diffusion of Zn from soils to plant roots.
- quantity-intensity relationship Zn – may be described by linear form of Langmuir type eqn.

$$\text{Supply Parameter} = qc^{1/2} \cdot K_1 K_2^{-1/4} \text{ or } \sqrt{\frac{cq}{\sqrt{K_1 K_2}}}$$

K_1 K_2 = constants.

Optimum Zn supply to rice when value of SP = 1.

Copper

- most of Cu in soils – very insoluble – can be extracted by strong chemical treatments – dissolve various mineral structures of solubilize organic matter.
- concn of Cu soil soln – very low.
- pH < 6.9 – Cu^{2+} dominant
- pH > 6.9 – $Cu(OH)_2^0$ – principal sp.
- pH – 7.0 – $CuOH^+$

Hydrolysis :–

$$Cu^{2+} + H_2O \rightleftharpoons CuOH^+ + H^+$$

$$CuOH^+ + H_2O \rightleftharpoons Cu(OH)_2^0 + H^+$$

$CuSO_4^0$ and $CuCO_3^0$ – imp. forms.

- solubility of Cu – pH dependent – ↑ 100 time – ↓ pH
- not involved in oxd- red reactions.
- Different pools:–
  a) water soluble + exc. Cu
  b) Cu associated with clay.
  c) Organically bound Cu
  d) Cu ass. with diff. oxides.
  e) Residual Cu.

$$\text{soil } Cu^{2+} + H^+ \rightleftharpoons Cu^{2+} \text{ (soluble)}$$

$$Cu_2(OH)_2CO_3 + 4H^+ \rightleftharpoons \underset{\text{(soluble)}}{Cu^{2+}} + CO_2 + 3H_2O$$

- chemical equilibria of Cu – similar to Zn.
- Acid soil – submergence – pH↑ – Cu↓ release of Cu↓

- alkali and calcareous — Cu soil soln ↑.
- Generally, sub. ↓ Cu and deficiency.

For (Increase)

- formation of organic complexes
- ↓pH (alkali soil)

(Decrease)

- Insoluble ppt as CuS, $CuCO_3$ and $Cu(OH)_2$ since prodn of sulphide, HCO_3^-, ~~an~~ CO_3 and OH more in sub.

- In soil with high OM — ↑ or ↓ - ~~or~~ contradictory

(Decrease)

- Microbiological immob.
- antagonistic effect of ↑ concn of Fe, Mn and P — insoluble complexes

(Increase)

- redn of coating of hydrous oxides of Fe^{3+} and Mn^{4+} on copper compounds and
- prodn of soluble Cu-organic chelates

Boron and Molybdenum

oxyanionic forms of B and Mo

- very much depend – pH, OM content, clay content
- ~~At~~ Acid soil – submerged — ↑ amt of Mo content – initially ↓ later period – almost unchanged

due to ↑ soil pH and desorption of MoO_4^{2-} from oxides and hydroxides of Fe and Mn.

- B in soil soln remain more or less constant after submer.

- H_2O retained at low matric suction (say 0–100 kPa)
  ↓
  depends on capillarity and pore size distribution.
  ↓
  so, strongly affected by soil's structure.
- At higher suctions, - water retention - due to adsorption so— soil's texture and specific surface.
- So, ↑ clay content - greater water retention at any part suction
  & ↙
  more gradual the slope of curve.
- In sandy soil - soil pores - relatively large - small amt remains
- In clayey soil - more water adsorbed - increasing matric suction ⟶ causes gradual decrease in wetness.

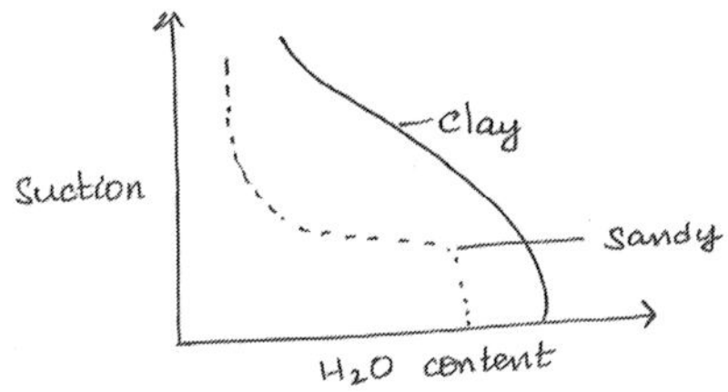

Effect of texture on soil-H_2O retention

- Compaction:-
  soil structure - influences shape of SMC primarily in low-suction range.
- compaction ⟶ destroys aggregated structure - ~~ree~~ ↓ porosity and ↓ volume of large interaggregate pores.
  so, saturation H_2O content and initial decrease of H_2O content with application of low suction are diminished.
- But, vol. of intermediate size pores ⟶ greater compact soil.
  ↓
  large pores - squeezed - intermediate size and micropores remain unaffected.
  So, curves of compacted & uncompacted soil - tend to converge in high suction range ⟵

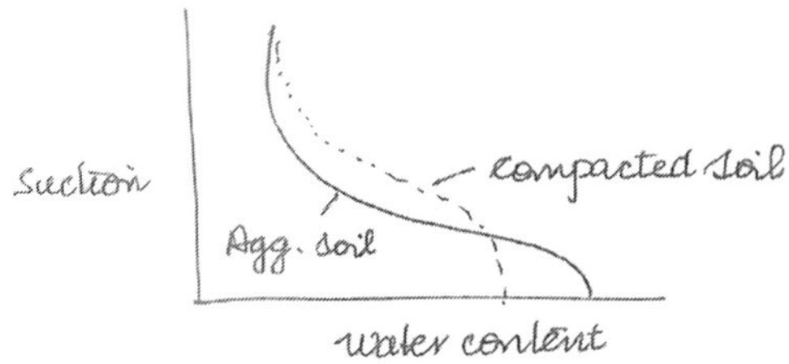

- If two soil bodies (differing in text. struct. initial wetness)
  ↓
  direct physical contact
  ↓
  even at equil^m – they will not have equal wetness
  ↓
  their content of H_2O determine by its own soil moisture characteristic.

- slope of SMCC — $\frac{\text{change of } \theta}{\text{change of } \Phi_p}$ = differential (specific) water capacity. C_θ

$C_\theta = \frac{d\theta}{d\Phi_p}$ or — matric potential

$C_\theta = -\frac{d\theta}{d\psi}$ — matric suction

↓ analogous to differential heat capacity = $\frac{dH}{d\Phi_T}$ — heat content

$= \frac{dH}{dT}$ — thermal potential (Temperature)

fairly constant

But strongly dependent on matric pot.

HYSTERESIS

- Relation between matric pot. and soil wetness – 2 ways:–
  a) desorption – initially saturated sample – apply increasing suction – stepwise manner – gradually dry – take successive measurements of wetness versus suction

b) sorption — gradually wetting up an initially dry soil sample — while reducing suction incrementally.

— ~~B~~ Two continuous curves are generated — but are different.

- equil^m soil wetness at given suction > in desorption > ~~ad~~sorption.

↓

This leads to hysteresis

- Causes: -

a) geometric nonuniformity of individual pores (- generally irregular shaped voids interconnected by smaller passages) — resulting 'ink bottle effect'.

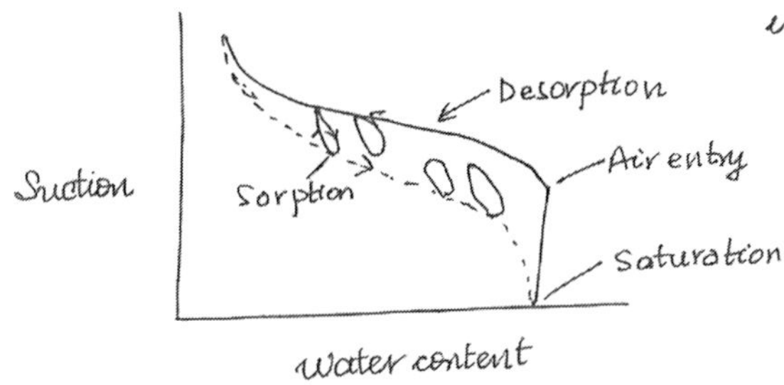

intermediate loops = scanning curves.

b) contact angle effect — contact angle is greater and hence radius of curvature > advancing meniscus than receeding. So, given H_2O content — exhibit greater suction in desorption. contact-angle hysteresis - can arise - because of surface roughness, presence of adsorbed impurities on solid surf → and mechanism by which liquid mol. adsorb or desorb when interface is displaced.

c) Entrapped air - further decreases water content of newly wetted soil.

d) Swelling, shrinking or ageing phenomena → result in differential changes in soil structure ~~dep~~..

INK-BOTTLE EFFECT

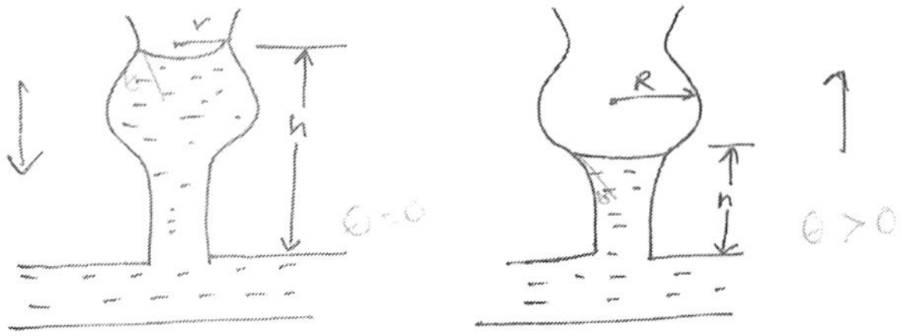

a) in capillary drainage (desorption)   b) in capillary rise (sorption)

equilibrium ht. of H_2O in a variable width pore

- desorption depends on — narrow radii of connecting channels
- sorption " " — larger pores.
- discontinuous spurts of H_2O — Haines jumps (after WB Haines — 1930)
  ↓
  observed readily in coarse sand
  ↓
  hysteresis effect more pronounced on coarse textured in low suction. ~~where~~

- Hysteretic soil-moisture charact.
  ↓
  Two main branches
  - gradual transition from saturation to dryness
  - dryness to saturation

- when partially wetted soil — drain or partially desaturated soil — rewetted — relation of suction to MC follows some intermediate curves — as it scans from one ~~branch~~ branch to another
  ↓
  scanning curves.
  ↓
  Cyclic changes often entail wetting and drying scanning curves — form loops between main branches.

So, because - of this complexity - hysteresis — ignored.

↓

So, soil moisture charac - commonly called - desorption curve

- sorption curve - equally important - but more difficult

Measurement of Soil Moisture Potential

- measurement of soil wetness alone - not sufficient - describing state of soil water.

- evaluation of energy status of soil H_2O necessary

↓

- total soil moist. pot = matric pot + osmotic (solute) pot usually taken

- matric + gravit (elevation) heads = hydraulic head/pot → useful in evaluating directions and magnitudes of water moving forces throughout soil profile.

- Matric pot → measured by Tensiometer — in field
  → in lab - tension plates and air - pressure extraction cells.

- Total soil moist pot → by measuring equilm vapour pressure of soil water by thermocouple psychrometer.

☆ Tensiometer

- provide continuous indication of soil's matric suction (or tension) in situ.

- consists of - porous cup (generally ceramic material).
  ↓
  connected through a tube to manometer — with all parts filled with H_2O

- when cup - placed in soil - bulk water inside cup comes into hydraulic contact - tends to equilibrate with soil water through the pores in ceramic walls.

- When tensiometer is placed - initially - water in it - at atm. pressure

- But soil water - sub atm. pressure - so → suction → draws out certain of amt from tensio - so causing pressure in tensiometer fall below atm. pressure.

subpressure inside tensiometer
↓
indicated by manometer, vacuum gauge / electrical transducer.

– tensiometer – kept in place – track the changes in soil's matric suction.
↓
soil moisture – depleted → by drainage or plant uptake
– replenish – rain or irrigation
} → corresponding readings.
↓
So, hydraulic resist. between cup and ~~soil and~~ surrounding soil
↓
contact zone between cup and soil
↓
tensiometer response may lag behind suction changes.
↓
can be minimized by using null type device or a transducer type manometer with rigid tubing
↙
so no flow of H_2O takes place.

– Since walls of porous cup – permeable to both water and solutes
↓
solutes in soil soln diffuse freely into porous cup, so water inside tensiometer – assume solute concn and composition as soil water.
↓
Therefore, instrument doesn't indicate osmotic suction of soil water.

- limited to matric suction values < 1 atm (1 bar or 100kPa)

Reasons:-

- vacuum gauge or manometer – measures partial vacuum relative to external atm. pressure.

↳ even if gauging of pressure independent of atm. pressure – still facing problem of water columns in macroscopic systems –

But water in narrow capillaries can maintain continuity at much higher tensions. – eg. continuity of water in xylem vessels of tall trees.

- ceramic cup – generally made of – permeable & porous mat – (to maintain rapid equilm with soil H_2O) → higher suction may cause entry of air from soil to cup. → equalizes the internal tensiometric pressure to atm. pressure.

↓

So, soil suction may continue to increase even – tensio. fails to show.

- Practically useful limit of tensi – 0.8 atm (80 kPa)

↓

But not a serious problem.

Reason:- 0 – 0.8 atm :– actually includes greater part of soil wetness range.

- In tension range – accounts for >50% (and for coarse text >75%) in agricult. soils of available soil water to plants.

- So, where soil management (like irrigation) – aiming at maintaining low suction condition (most favourable for plant growth) – in this case, tensiometers are mostly useful.

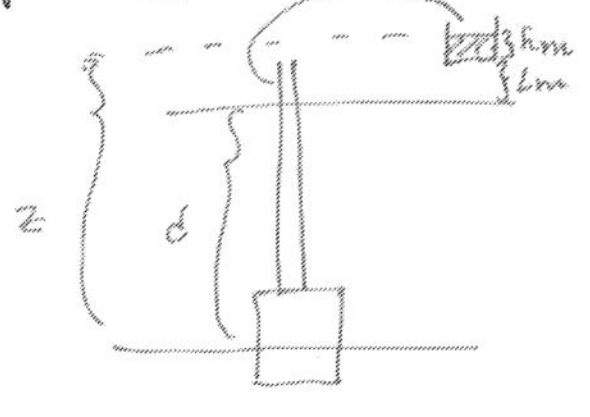

– Thermocouple Psychrometer

$$\Psi_m = \frac{-13.6 \times h_m}{\rho_w} + z$$

(13.6 = dens. of Hg; ρ_w = density of H_2O)

hm = ht of mercury of manometer

Lm = ht from surface

z = (d + lm + hm)

z = depth – rise of mercury from mano. to mid pt of porous cup.

Measurement of Soil-Moisture charac. curve

- relation between – soil wetness and matric suction –
through tension plate assembly — 1 bar (100 kPa)/1 atm
↳ $<$ 1 bar range (low suction)
- pressure plate or pressure membrane apparatus
↳ higher suction

allow appln of successive suction values and repeated measurement of soil wetness at such suction.

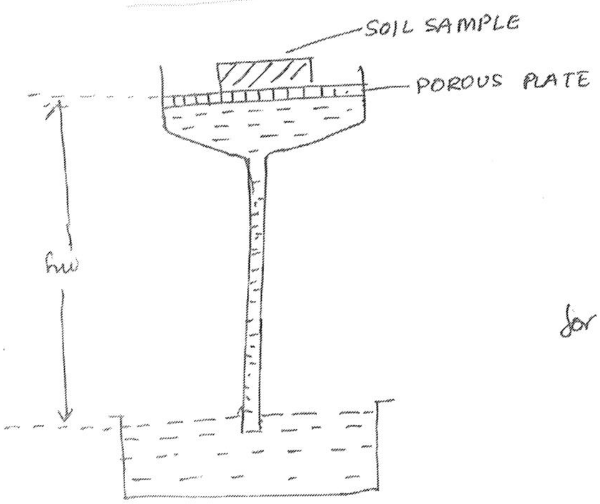

for 0 – 1 bar

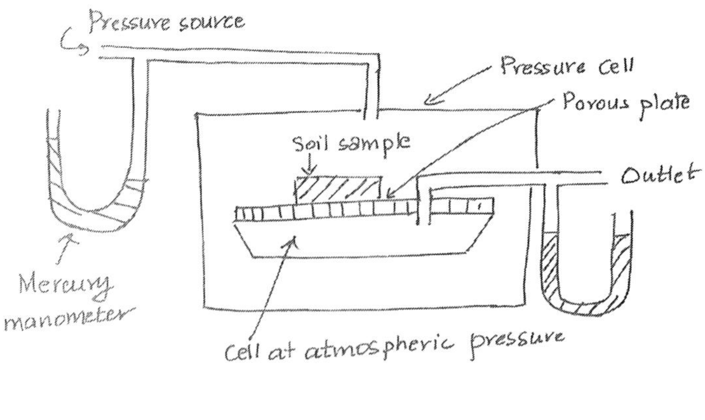

- if soil is kept at atm. pressure — ~~pressure~~ tension plate
- if pressure diff. across plate controlled by vacuum or by hanging H_2O column — tension plate
- So, matric suction > 1 bar — can be obtained by ↑ pressure of air phase – so, it requires placing porous plate assembly inside pressure chamber. – so, limit of matric suction — determined ~~by~~ design of chamber ~~and by~~
- Soil moisture suction – in low suction — strongly influenced by soil structure and pore size distribution.

↳ so, measurements using disturbed sample → can't represent field cond.

↓ so, undisturbed soil cores. preferred.

- Remote sensing of surface zone soil moisture.

Contd
Tensiometer

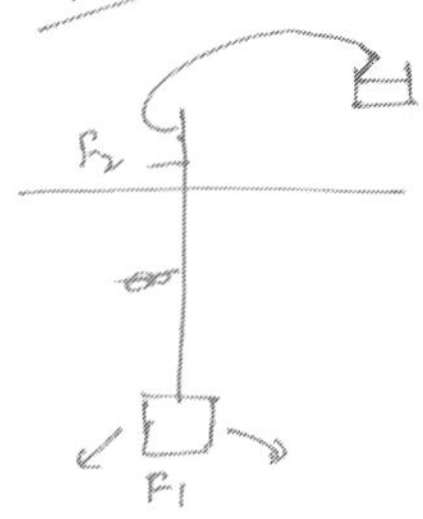

F_1 = force due to soil taking H_2O from porous cup
F_2 = force due to standing H_2O in tube
F_3 = force " " rising of mercury

$$F_1 - F_2 = -F_3$$

$$\Rightarrow m_1 g - m_2 g = -m_3 g$$

$$\Rightarrow V_1 \rho_w g - V_2 \rho_w g = -V_3 \rho_{Hg} \cdot g$$

$$\Rightarrow (V_1 \rho_w - V_2 \rho_w) g = -V_3 \rho_{Hg} g$$

$$\Rightarrow \frac{V_1 \rho_w}{a} - \frac{V_2 \rho_w}{a} = -\frac{V_3 \rho_{Hg}}{a}$$

[since $\frac{vol}{area}$ = ht]

$$\Rightarrow \rho_w \cdot h - \rho_w \cdot z = -\rho_{Hg} \cdot hm$$

$$\Rightarrow \rho_w (h - z) = -\rho_{Hg} \cdot hm$$

$$\Rightarrow h - z = -\frac{\rho_{Hg} \cdot hm}{\rho_w}$$

$$\Rightarrow h = -\frac{\rho_{Hg} \cdot hm}{\rho_w} + z$$

↓
ψ_m

WATER FLOW IN SATURATED SOIL

LAMINAR FLOW IN NARROW TUBES

- Earlier – assumption - perfect fluid – frictionless and incompressible – contacting layers no tangential forces (shearing stresses)
- But in real fluids – tangential stresses (drag) and intermolecular attraction causes molecules in contact with a solid wall to adhere to it.
- real fluid - associated with viscosity.

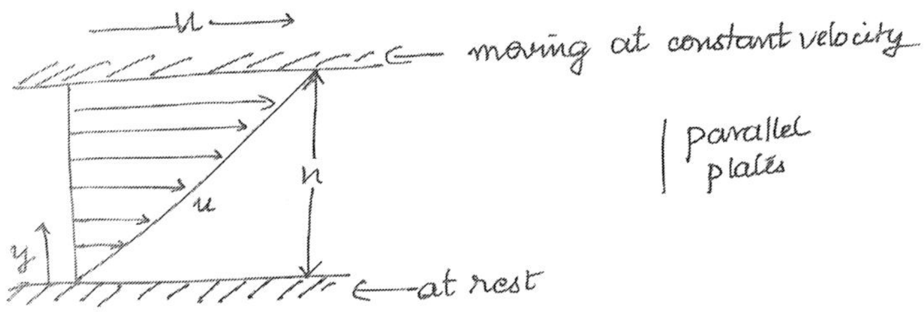

- velocity at lower plate = 0 and at upper plate velocity = velocity of plate (as fluid adheres to both walls)
- veloc. distribution in fluid between two plates → linear
- fluid velocity at any plane between plates ∝ dist. y from lower plate

- Laminar flow prevails at – low flow velocity and in narrow tubes.
- As radius of tube and flow velocity ↑ – mean flow velocity at a point – no longer proportional to pressure drop – parallel laminar flow changes into a turbulent flow with fluctuating eddies.

★ DARCY'S LAW

- of soil- bundle of straight and narrow smooth tubes (uniform radius) → overall flow rate = sum of separate flows through individual tubes.
- So, if we know size distribution of tube radii – then we can calculate total flow caused by a known press. difference – by Poiseuille's equation.
- But in soil – irregular shaped, tortuous and intricately interconnected tubes — so restricted flow.

↓

fluid veloci. varies from point to point even along same passage

↓

so, actual geometry and flow pattern in soil – too complicated to be described in microscopic detail

↓

so described in macroscopic flow velocity vector

↓

overall average of microscopic velocities over total volume considered.

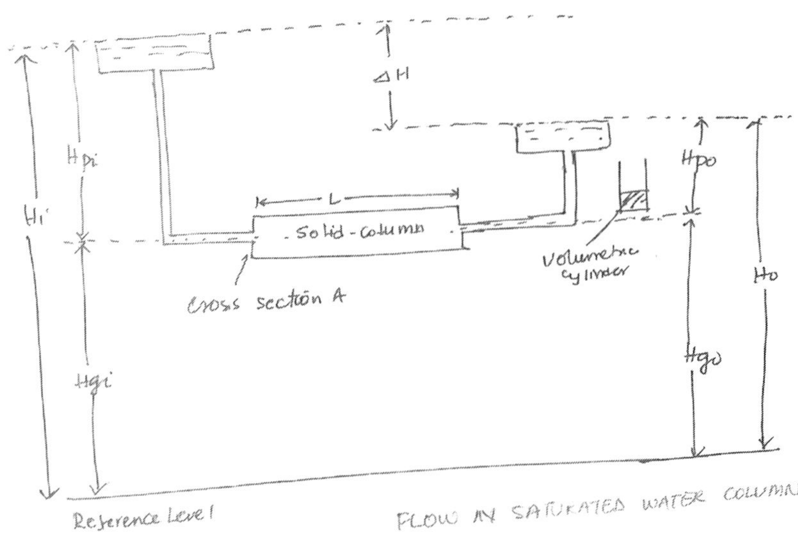

FLOW IN SATURATED WATER COLUMN

- fig - flow of H_2O in macroscopically uniform, saturated soil body ~~and attempt~~ I

- steady flow of H_2O flowing through column from an upper reservoir - ~~in~~ to lower one - each of their water level maintained constant.

- Discharge rate Q (volume v flowing through column per unit time)
  - ↳ ∝ cross-sec. area.
  - ↳ ∝ hydraulic head drop ΔH
  - ↳ $\frac{1}{\propto}$ length of column L → measure head at inflow boundary H_i and outflow bo. H_o relative to some ref. level.

$Q = \frac{V}{t}$.

$Q \propto \frac{A \Delta H}{L}$

$\boxed{\Delta H = H_i - H_o}$

In absence of hydraulic head diff. ie when $\Delta H = 0$ → no flow.

- So, ΔH (head drop) per unit distance in the direction of flow, ie $\frac{\Delta H}{L}$ = hydraulic gradient → driving force.

- Specific discharge rate $\frac{Q}{A}$ (vol. of H_2O flowing through a unit cross sec - area per unit time t) = flux density → q

$q \propto$ hydraulic grad.

$q = \frac{Q}{A}$

$= \frac{V}{At} \propto \frac{\Delta H}{L}$

$q \propto \frac{\Delta H}{L}$

Assumptions:

i) negligible KE of H_2O — when flow vel. small as compared to PE
ii) constant mass density of H_2O } valid as long as temp doesn't change.
iii) constant visco. of H_2O
iv) streamline flow when flow vel < critical vel ~~for~~. As flow vel ↑ - turbulent

$\boxed{\Rightarrow q = K \frac{\Delta H}{L}}$ — Darcy's Law

↳ proportionality factor K = hydraulic conductivity.

- after Henry Darcy – French engineer – discovered over a ~~century ago in~~ during classic investigation of seepage rates through sand filters in the clay of Dijon.

- Dijon – city – known for mustard prodn – pungent wastes of the industry – fouling of city's H_2O supply – Henry Darcy – to design a filtration system.

- Why Darcy's law is – differential form?
  - ↳ where – flow – unsteady
  - where – soil – nonuniform

  } → hydraulic head may not ↓ linearly along the direction of flow.

- so must consider instantaneous localized gradient, those and conductivity values rather than avg. values of soil system as a whole.

- Slichter (1899) generalized – D's Law – into 3 dimensional macroscopic differential eqn.

$q = -K.\nabla H$ ↳ 3 d. gradient of hyd. head.

↓ product of scalar(K) vector (∇H) } → q = vector so direction determined by ∇H.

Postulation

flow of a viscous liquid – through a porous medium – in the direction of, and proportional to, driving force acting on the liquid (ie hydraulic gradient) and also ∝ transmitting property of conducting medium (H c).

- Mathematically – Darcy's law – similar to – Ohm's Law.

  ↓ Current / flow rate of electr. ∝ ΔE

- Fourier's law – rate of heat conduction ∝ ΔT

- Fick's Law – diffusion rate ∝ ΔC.

GRAVITATIONAL, PRESSURE AND TOTAL HYDR-HEADS

- water entering the column in fig - under pressure
- since atm pressure same on both ends of the system → disregard and consider only hydrostatic pressure. ↳ Hydrostatic press + atmospheric pressure on surface of H_2O.
- At inflow boundary, water pressure $P_i = \rho_w g H_{pi}$ → nearly constant so
- Water flow - in horizontal - in response to a pressure head gradient. $P_i = H_{pi}$ ↳ Pressure head.
- For vertical - gravitation + pressure.
- Hg (grav. head) at any point = ht of pt. relative to some ref. plane.
- H_{pi} = ht. of H_2O column resting on that point.
- Total hydraulic head $H = H_g + H_p$.
- If Darcy's law → vertical flow → must consider total hydr. head at inflow and outflow → $H_i + H_o$.

$$H_i = H_{pi} + H_{gi}$$
$$H_o = H_{po} + H_{go}$$

So, Darcy's Law thus becomes

~~$q = K\nabla H$~~

$$q = K\frac{H}{L}$$
$$= K\frac{[(H_{pi} + H_{gi}) - (H_{po} + H_{go})]}{L}$$

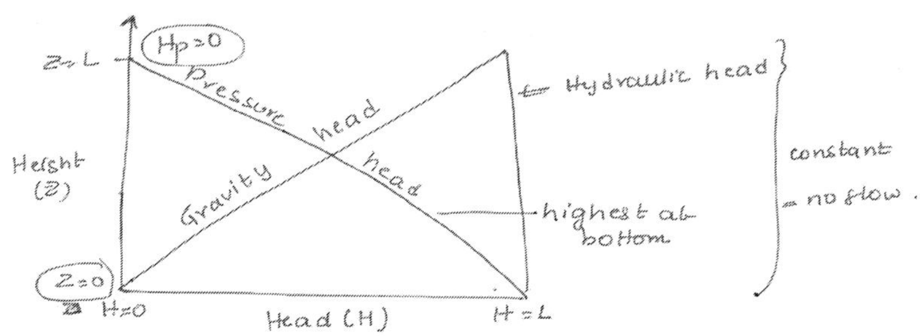

Minimum hydraulic head = 0

Maxm = L

– immerse and equilibrate a vert. soil column in H_2O reservoir

↓

upper surface of column – level with H_2O surface

–  ht. above the bottom of column – indicated by z, vert. axis

pressure, gravity, hydraulic head – hori. axis.

– The gravity head increases with ht at 1:1 ratio.

– Pressure head determined with ref. to free water surface – where hydrostatic pressure = 0.

– at surface – hydro. pressure = 0

bottom – = L

so, as grav head ↑, pressure head ↓, ✓

↓

sum = hydraulic head – remains constant all along the column – state of equi/m – no flow occurs.

↓

Further explaination

– water pressure not constant along the column

↓

greater in bottom ~~but~~ than at top.

↓

Then why flow – from zone of higher pressure to low pressure not takes place).

↓

It can be flowing in horizontal column – where no gra. gradi.

↓

But in vertical – opposing pres. gravitati. gradient of equal magnitude – water at top – higher gr. potential than at bottom.

↓

so cancel each other → Total hydraulic head = constant

↓

measured by piezometers.

- So, convenient – to set – ref level at bottom of column so that grav. pot = always +ve.

On other hand – pressure head = +ve / –ve — above H_2O surface.
↓
under free H_2O surface (H_2O table)

FLOW IN VERT. COLUMN

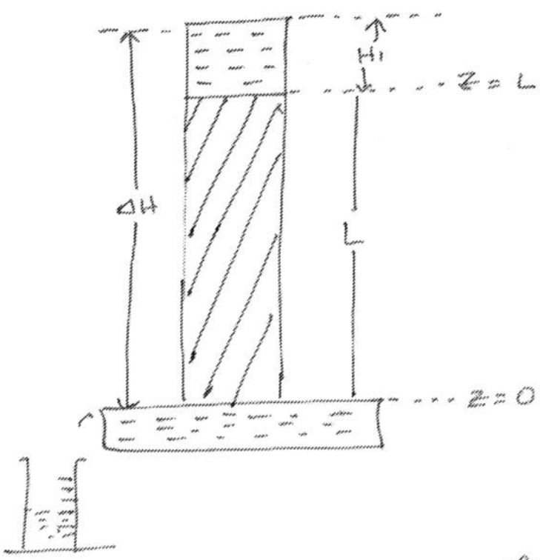

- uniform sat. vert. column – upper surface – ponded under a constant head of water H_1 and bottom surface — set in lower, constant level reservoir.
↓
flow is taking place through column of L length.

To know the flux using Darcy's law – we must know hydraulic head gradient = $\frac{\text{hydraulic head drop between inflow and outflow}}{\text{Length}}$.

	Pressure head	+	Gravity head	Hydraulic head
Inflow boundary	H_1	+	L	$= H_1 + L$
Outflow	0	+	0	$= 0 + 0$

$$\Delta H = H_i - H_o = H_1 + L$$

Darcy's equation for this case: –

$$q = K\frac{\Delta H}{L}$$

$$= K\frac{(H_1 + L)}{L} = \frac{K H_1}{L} + K$$

In case of horizontal,

$$q = K\frac{\Delta H}{L}.$$

Comparing vert and hort. flow — rate of downward flow in vertical column > horizontal column — by magnitude of Hc. If H1 (ponding depth) is negligible

↓

flux = ~~lo~~ K

In absence of pressure gradient — only driving force = gravitational head gradient —but→ has value of unity (as grav. ~~gr~~ head varies with height in 1:1)

– In case of upward flow — directn of flow opp. to direction of grav. gradient.

~~In~~

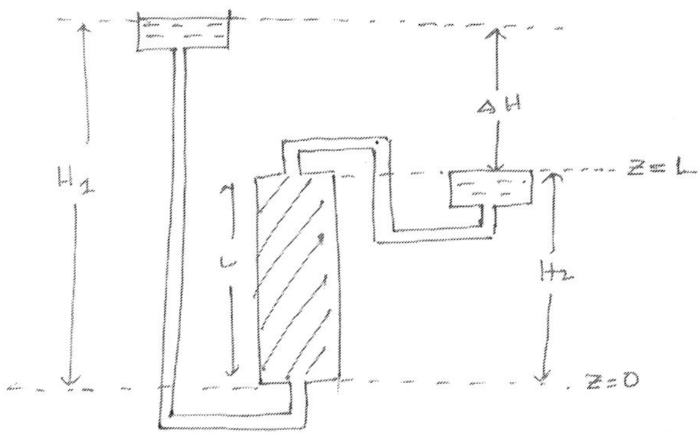

So, hydraulic gradient becomes

			Pressure head		Gravity head
Hy. head at inflow	H_i	=	H_1	+	0
,, ,, ,, outflow	H_o	=	0	+	L
Hydraulic head diff.	$\Delta H = H_i - H_o$	=	H_1	−	L

So, Darcy's eqn.

$$q = \frac{K(H_1 - L)}{L} = K\frac{\Delta H}{L}$$

FLUX, FLUX VELOCITY, TORTUOSITY

- flux density / flux

volume of H_2O 'V' passing through cross unit cross-sec area 'A' (⊥r to flow of direction) per unit time 't'.

dimensions

$$q = \frac{V}{At} = \frac{L^3}{L^2T} = LT^{-1}$$

In SI unit $= \frac{m^3}{m^2\,sec} = m\,sec^{-1}$

prefer flux to flux velocity ↳ too ambiguous.

- Tortuosity

$$= \frac{\text{average roundabout path}}{\text{apparent (straight) flow path}}$$

$$= \frac{\text{average length of pore passages}}{\text{length of soil specimen.}}$$

- dimensionless
- always > 1, may exceed 2
- Tort. factor → Inverse.

HYDRAULIC CONDUCTIVITY, PERMEABILITY AND FLUIDITY

→ HYDRAULIC CONDUC, $K = \frac{\text{flux}}{\text{potential gradient}}$ ie slope of flux vs Pot-gr.

- dimension → LT^{-1} (same as flux)
  ↳ depend on that of pot. grad.
- simplest way to express potential – by use of length / head though H is not a true length – but pressure equivalent in terms of water column $H = \frac{P}{\rho g}$

↳ so, $\frac{H}{L}$ hydraulic head gradient $= \frac{H}{L} = \frac{\text{length}}{\text{length}}$ = dimensionless.

- But if gradient expressed — in terms of variation of hydraulic pressure with length → HC → $M^{-1}L^{3}T$. — but cumbersome.

- In saturated soil of stable structure, rigid porous medium (sandstone) — HC — nearly constant → 10^{-4}–10^{-5} m/sec (sandy soil)

10^{-6}–10^{-9} m/sec (clayey)

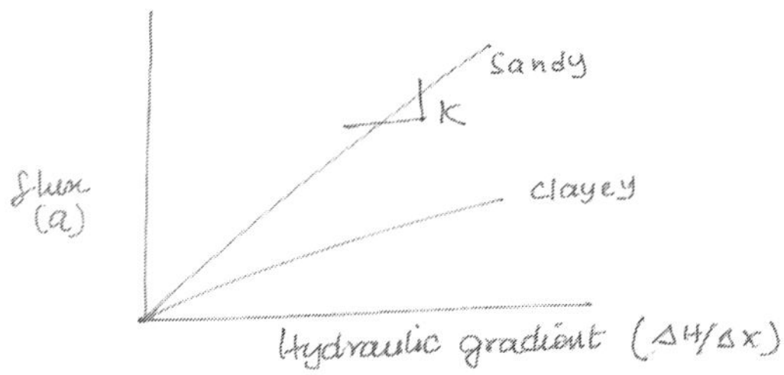

- linear dependence of flux on Hy. gradient, HC being the slope.

- Factors affecting HC
  - structure, texture
  - sizes of conducting pores.
  - HC of saturated soil often vary (generally diminishes over time)

Reason

- Changes in composition of the water — .
- HC ↓ with ↓ concn of electrolytic solutes → due to swelling and dispersion phenomena — also affected by species of cation. Detachment and migration of clay part — clogging of pores.

- Encapsulated air bubbles block pore passages
- Temp. changes — cause flowing water to dissolve or release gas bubbles — also cause change in volume — affecting HC.

- HC not a property of soil alone — depends jointly on soil + fluid attributes.

Soil attributes : total porosity, distribution of pore sizes and tortuosity. — (soil's pore geometry)

fluid attribut : density, viscosity

- In theory, sometimes in practice to separate HC < two factors: Intrinsic perm. of soil (k); fluidity of permeating liquid/gas (f)

$$K = kf$$

If $K = m/sec\ (LT^{-1})$

then $k = m^2\ (L^2)$

and $f = m^{-1} sec^{-1}\ (L^{-1}T^{-1})$

- $f \rightarrow \propto$ density but $\frac{1}{\propto}$ viscosity → Nsec/m² or Pa.sec.

$$f = \frac{\rho g}{\eta}$$

(ρ → kg/m³, g → m/sec²)

Hence,

$$K = kf$$

$$\Rightarrow K = k\frac{\rho g}{\eta}$$

$$\Rightarrow k = \frac{K\eta}{\rho g}$$

while fluidity (varies) — with temp and composition.

- Intrinsic Per — ideally a property of porous medium's pore geometry alone.

provided both dnot interact so that it change the prop. of either.

↓

But mostly - interact — so, can't separate.

LIMITATIONS OF DARCY's LAW

- Darcy's Law - not universally valid for all conditions of liquid flow in porous media.

- linearity of flux vs hydraulic gradient relationship - fails at high flow velocities

↳ where inertial forces - no longer negligible compared to viscous forces. —

— applies only to laminar flow (non turbulent movement of adjacent layers of the fluid relative to one another)

— applies where soil-water interctn doesn't result — change of fluidity or k with change in gradient.

— Laminar flow — prevails — silts and finer mat

— In coarse sands — Hydraulic gradients — much in excess of unity — non laminar flow — So, Darcy's law not appli.

— Quantitative criterion for onset of turbulent flow

Reynolds no, N_{Re}:

$$N_{Re} = \frac{dv\rho}{\eta}$$

- d — effective pore diameter
- v — mean flow velocity
- ρ — liquid density
- η — viscosity

— In straight tubes — critical value of N_{Re} — beyond which turbulence sets in → 1000–2200 order.

But it is lesser than this when tube-curved and its diameter varies.

So, for porous media, it is safe to assume — flux remains linear with hy. gradient only as long as $N_{Re} < 1$

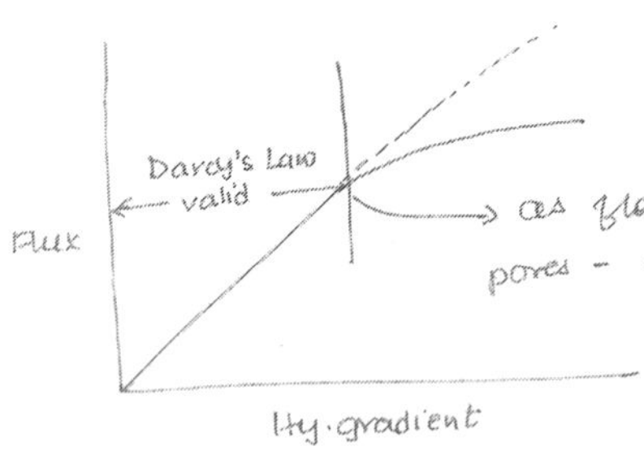

→ as flow vel. ↑ in case of large pores — turbulent eddies — waste of effective energy
↓
hydraulic pot grad. becomes less effective in inducing flow.

— Deviations from Darcy's law — not only at high-flow vel. but also at other opposite end of flow-velocity range — ie low gradients and in narrow pores.

↓

Clay soil – small hydraulic grad. → no flow or only low flow rates — less than ∝ to grad.

↓

Reason

① – adsorptive forces – more. — water near to the particle surfaces — may exhibit properties of a Bingham liquid. (having yield value)
– adsorbed H_2O – may even have a quasi-crystalline structure ↳ similar to ice.

(ii) tendency to swell or compress of clay

↓

Darcy's law applied to geometrically fixed porous matrix and it may seem to fail when particles are themselves moving.

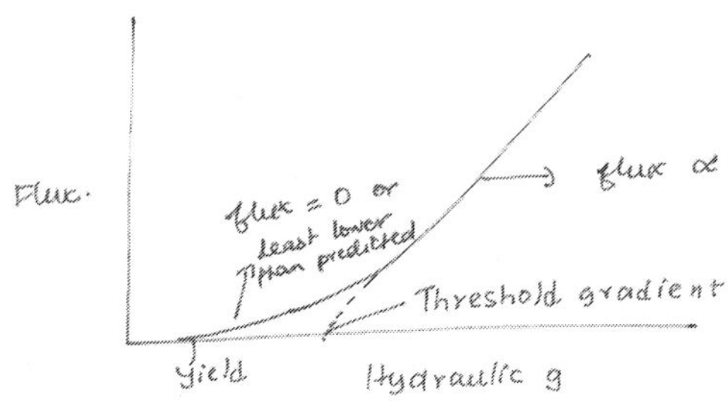

→

MEASURING HC OF SAT. SOIL

- In Laboratory – permeameters
- Field measure – auger hole method / piezometer
  – field permeameter.

- Constant head permeameter
- Falling " "

EQUATIONS FOR SAT. FLOW

- Darcy's Law – for steady, stationary flow.
- Unsteady or transient flow – magnitude and direction of flux and pot. gradient vary with time.

↓

so, need inclusion of law of consew. of matter

↓

Consider a small vol. element (cube) of soil – into and out flow takes place.

- Law of cons. of mass – expressed in the eqn of continuity –
if rate of inflow into the volume element > rate of outflow – then vol. element must be storing excess and ↑ its H_2O content.
If outflow > inflow – storage must be decreasing.

- q_x = flux in 'x' direction.
So, any ↑ q_x ⇒ ↓ water content w with time t

$$\frac{d\theta}{dt} = -\frac{dq_x}{dx}$$

$$-\frac{dq_x}{dx} = \frac{d\theta}{dt} \quad \text{(one dimens)}$$

Multidimensional

$$\frac{d\theta}{dt} = -\nabla q \quad \text{———} \quad (1)$$

Darcy's Law

~~$q = K\nabla$~~

$q = -K\nabla H$ —— (2)

$q_x = -K\left(\frac{dH}{dx}\right)$ —— (2) (hydraulic head; HC)

Combining (1) + (2)

$$\frac{d\theta}{dt} = -\nabla q$$

$$q = -K\nabla H$$

$$\Rightarrow \frac{d\theta}{dt} = \nabla K \nabla H \quad [\text{General flow eq}^n]$$

Assumptions

(i) Here, inertial forces – assumed – negligible as comp-to viscous forces.

(ii) H_2O continuously connected throughout flow region

(iii) isothermal condition

(iv) no ~~change~~ in chemical / biolog. phenomena – change fluid or porous medium during flow process.

$$\frac{d\theta}{dt} = \frac{d}{dx}\left[K \cdot \frac{dH}{dx}\right]$$

partial differential eq^n with 2 independ. variable t, x

Since hydraulic head → resolved → into pressure head H_p and a gravitational head (an elevat^n z above some ref. datum)

$$\frac{d\theta}{dt} = \nabla K \nabla H$$

$$\frac{d\theta}{dt} = \nabla\left[K(\nabla H_p + \nabla z)\right]$$

In horizontal flow, $\nabla z = 0$, so for this case,

$$\frac{d\theta}{dt} = \frac{d}{dx}\left[K\left(\frac{\partial H_p}{dx}\right)\right]$$

For vertical flow $\frac{dz}{dz} = 1$, so.

$$\frac{d\theta}{dt} = \frac{d}{dz}\left[K\left(\frac{dH_p}{dz} + 1\right)\right]$$

- In sat. soil with an incompressible matrix, $\frac{d\theta}{dt} = 0$. The conductivity usually assumed to remain constant.

So, $K_s = \frac{\partial^2 H}{\partial x^2} = 0$

(K_s — HC of sat. soil)

For 3-D

$$K_x \frac{d^2 H}{dx^2} + K_y \frac{d^2 H}{dy^2} + K_z \frac{d^2 H}{dz^2} = 0$$

K_x, K_y, K_z — HC in 3 principal directions x, y, z

- In isotropic soil (where $K_x = K_y = K_z$ at each point) — which is also homogeneous — Laplace eq^n

$$\frac{\partial^2 H}{\partial x^2} + \frac{\partial^2 H}{\partial y^2} + \frac{\partial^2 H}{\partial z^2} = 0$$

→ in quantitative description of steady-state flows.

→ 2nd order partial diff. eq^n of elliptical type

WATER FLOW IN UNSATURATED SOIL

Difference between unsaturated and saturated

- In unsaturated soil → most of the processes involving soil-water interactions in field. ~~whereas~~ Unsaturated flow - generally complicated and difficult to quantify - since they often entail changes in state and content of soil H_2O during flow.
- Flow of H_2O - driven by hydraulic pot. gradient - apply both to sat and unsat. soil → but nature of moving force and effective geometry of the conducting pores may be different
- apart from gravitational force (→ completely independent of soil wetness), - primary moving force in sat soil - gradient of +ve pressure pot.

  but in unsaturated soil - sub atm. pressure or matric suction
  ↓
  = -ve pressure pot.
- Matric suction - physical affinity between H_2O and matric of soil.
  ↓
  If matric suction = uniform along a horizontal column of soil
  ↓
  column is at equil^m
  ↓
  no moving force.
- But when suction gradient exists, water will flow from
  - from zone ~~where~~ thicker hydration envelope to thinner
  - zone of less curved capillary menisci to more strongly curved.
  - from lower matric suction to higher matric suction.
- Ideal state of equil^m - never achieved in practice.
- HC - most imp difference - when saturated - HC maximal (all pores are water filled and conducting)

  ↳ So, when soil desaturates - some air filled - conductive portion of soil's cross-sec area ↓.
  ↓
  ~~And when~~ as suction develops - the first pores to empty → largest ones - which are most conducting (acc to Poiseuille's Law)

- So, tortuosity ↑.
- So, transition from sat → unsat → steep drop in HC.

RELATION OF CONDUCTIVITY TO SUCTION AND WETNESS

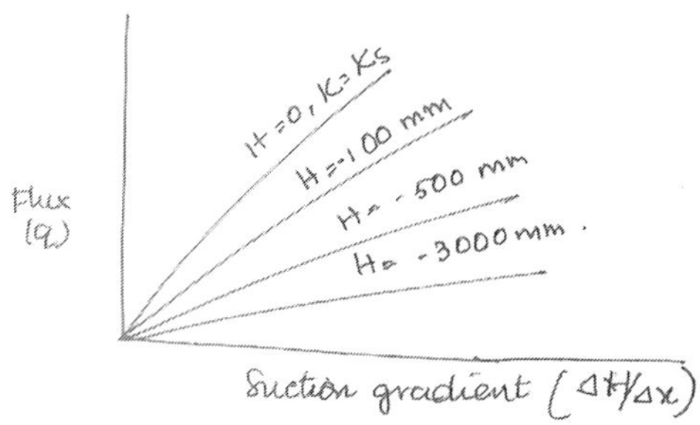

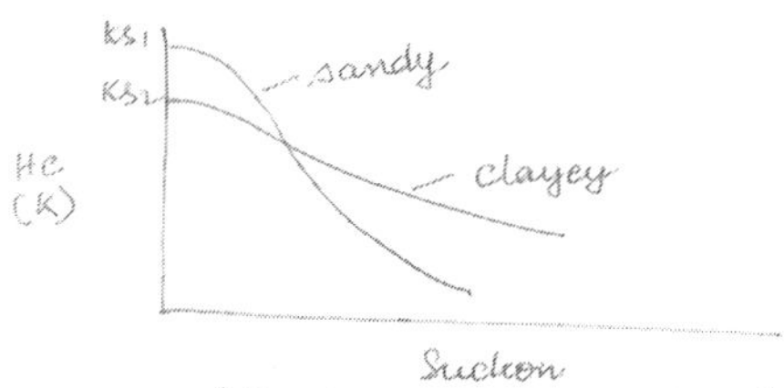

↑ Dependence of K on suction in diff soils.

Kv. K vs suction — drawn on log-log scale because k and ψ vary over several orders of magnitude within the suction range of general interest.

∴ Saturated conductivity of sandy soil Ks1 > clayey soil Ks2.

But unsaturated cond — Ks1 — decreases — more steeply with ↑ suction and becomes lower.

- Steep decline of HC with rising matric suction — suggests that processes taking part in wet soil conditions — faster than those in drier regions.

↓

- So, infiltration — more rapid than evaporation.
  infiltration: moves into soil profile
  evaporation: moves out from soil.

Management of soil Phy. Quality

- maintaining soil quality – to meet increasing demands.
- 3 mutually interactive attributes – phy, che and biolo.
- soil phy. quality – ability of a given soil – to meet plant and ecosystem requirements for water, aeration and strength over time and to resist and recover from processes that diminish that ability.
  (must be restored to optimum to sustain productivity.)
- Physical envn – influences chemical and bio prop.
- ↳ nutrient and H_2O uptake, pollutant transport and emission of GHGs from soil.

Soil physical constraints

- out of 328 mha — 120.72 mha degraded — 89.52 mha (Phy)
  (< 20% of potential capacity)
- Sh. Surface crusting — 10.25 (load, nose) — Haryana, Punjab, WB
  temporary waterlogging — 6.24 (b. nor) — MP, Mahar, Punjab
  soil hardening — 21.57 Km — AP, Mah, Bihar
  Shallow depth — 26.40 mha — AP, Mahar, WB, Kerala
  sub-surface compacted layer — 11.31 — Mahar, Punjab, Bihar
  slow and high permeability — 13.75 — Rajas, WB, Gujarat
  (6)
- Physical problems – corrective measure – not available easily and cheaply.

Management options

TMRMFCA — Site specific need based feeding

- site specific technologies TMRMFCBA
- optimal use of tillage practices
- mulches
- Crop residues
- Manures
- Fertilizers.
- Appropriate cropping systems
- use of amendments like gypsum – sodic
  lime – acidic

4R – Right source, rate, time, place

Optimal use of tillage prac

- change phy, che, bio envn of soil
- either loosens or compacts the soil — change its vol-mass rela, changes clod size distribution, ↑ surface roughness, porosity, kill weeds
- affect soil-water regime, resistence to erosion, mechanical impedance, aeration status and soil temp.
- affect germination and root growth.

Types

Deep Tillage

- loosening of soil ↓, compaction ↑ → BD
- Deep tillage in Sandy → ↓BD of tilled zone as cmpd to conven. tilla.
- ↓BD → ↑ macropores — drain out H_2O rapidly — able to restore adequate water free porosity

No Tillage

- ↑BD of surface
- But gets mitigated — by retention of residue on surface — moderating effect of mulch.
- ↓ BD and ↑ porosity under no-till
- particularly for clayey — minimize subsoil compaction and induce structure formation through shrink-swell cycles

Conservation

- with residue layer on soil surface — checks -ve factors causing soil degradation
- ↑ soil aggregn — conserve soil moisture
- ↑ infiltration and moderates thermal regime
- But in humid temperate region — slow down soil warming process — cause impediment in sowing operations

- conserv. tillage results – more continuous pore system because ↑ in earthworm activity, old root channels and vertical cracks between peds.

- During wheat growth – in winter – ↑ minm soil temp by ~~0.5–2°c~~ 0.5–2°c and lowered maxm soil temp by 0.3–2°C at 5cm depth.

Appropriate cropp sy

- affect SOM content
- changes in physical pro – due to continuous cropping.
- wheat-corn-fallow – returning more residues to soil.
- impact of cropp. sy on BD and porosity is system specific.
- all tillage and crop manag. system → ↑ HC than fallow

Mulching

- artificial application of mat such as crop residues, plastic or paper on soil surface.
- influences soil moist. regime
  - by control. evaporam from soil surface
  - ↑ infiltration and soil moist. retention
  - facilitating condensation of H_2O at night due to temp reversals.
- ↓ evapor from soil surface by retarding intensity of radiation and wind vel.
- Orientation of residue – flat/matted, standing } – affects porosity and thickness of the layer
- Dry spell – mulch – keep surface moist – longer period – prolonged the first stage of evapor.
- under limited irrigation – rice husk – wheat
- Mulching + OM — barrier for runoff
- Mulch intercepts rainwater and protects from erosion

- prevents crust formation
- ↑ infiltration — more important in drought
- loss of H_2O through runoff ↓ exponentially with ↑ in mulch rate
- adequate quantity — mitigate effect of degree of slope in reducing runoff and soil loss.
- effective in wind erosion. →
- Standing crop residues — more eff.
  ↓ depends on plant density of the crop harvested and their size above the ground.
- ↑ soil temp during cooler weather
  ↓ hot spells.
- Organic mulches enhances soil temp — night, early morning.
  ↓ day time.
- Straw mulch – sugarcane → ↓ maxm soil temp
- Transparent polyethene → ↑ maxm " "
- Organic mulches → ↓ " "
- Black poly — doesn't alter maxm soil temp appreciably
- Gaseous comp. of soil air under mulch — depends on nature of mulch material (C : N), rate of decomp, soil mois. regime and climatic condition
- ↑ CO_2 build up – plastic — as film doesn't allow it to escape
- So, CO_2 comes through holes — chimney effect is created → localized concn of CO_2 for actively growing leaves — that ↑ photosynthesis — ↑ growth.
- → ↑ biological quality → ↑ soil structure
- MWD of water stable aggregates ↑.
- BD ↓ — ↑ earthworm acti.

Judicious use of Manures (OM) and mineral fertilizers

- Long Term exp - (LTFE) – FYM + fert – ↑ soil phy. health.
- through addn of OM
- fert → ↑ plant biomass → ↑ return of org. mat → ↑ SOM → ↓ BD → ↑ WHC, Infilt.
- But Magnitude – different – for soil, crop. HC sys, agroclimatic situation and doses of fert and manure use.
- NPK dose - optimum – 7-13 yrs – ↓ BD (slightly)
- BD further ↓ – when 10-15 t ha^{-1} FYM added along NPK.
- OM - main binding agent – water stability of soil - clay-humus complex.
- microbially mediated decomp - of OM – produces polymers – bind soil part – ↓ down rate of aggregate wetting.
- Phosphatic fert → ↑ aggregation – Al or Ca phosphate compounds
- where ↑ NH_4^+ concn → dispersion of colloids like Na^+
- Improves H_2O retention at lower suctions.

Management options

Highly permeable soil

- Light texture laterite and fluffy soils → ↑ permeability → loss of water and nutrients
- Technologies – compaction
  - clay addition
  - Compactn + clay add.

Compaction

- involves repeated passes of roller of sufficient wt drawn by animal or tractor at optimum soil moist content (Proctor moisture) to attain the desired level of compaction i.e. BD
- Level of compaction - specific – for specific soil - climate - crop combination → Most spectacular results – lateritic soils of WB and coastal sandy soil of TN

→ ↓ percolation loss of H_2O & nut.

Clay addn

- at 2% to red sandy loam AP → ↑ crop yield 10%
- ↳ Continuous addition for 2-3 yrs at same rate recommended
- Owing to formatn of stable aggregates, ↑ H_2O and nutrient retention by clay.
- viable where fine textured soil is available either from ponds or nearby fields and where economical to transport

Clay add + comp

- desired effect of comp – not obtained in desert without addn of clay.
- compaction + 2% clay.
- Desert Technology
- Increase yield – wheat (29%)
  Pearl millet (37%)
- low cost roller – Jobner-reinforced Fe concrete roller (JRIC roller)
  ↳ Rajasthan

Sub-surface ~~hardening~~ compacted layer

- restricts root growth and movement of air, H_2O and nutrients, which affects crop yield.

- Chisel Techno
- Chisel + amendm
- Ridge Tech

Chisel

- Deep tillage/chiselling breaks subsurface compaction
- chiselling upto 30-50 cm depth at 50-60 cm intervals.

- Residual effect of chiselling upto 7th successive crop — signif. in red soils — the effect diminish fast in light texture
  ↙
  so, chiselling — every rainy (kharif) — in light text.
  once in 2-3 yrs — in red soil.
- low cost chisel plough — Coimbatore

Chisel + amend

- Subsurf. comp — black soils — broken by chiseling — restore to compaction due to rapid swelling of montmor.
- Amend. like gypsum 5 $t ha^{-1}$ or FYM 20 $t ha^{-1}$ ↓ rate of comp.

Ridge Tech

- Rooting volume above compacted layer ↑.
- yield — Mustard (33%)
  Pearl millet (37%)

Hardening

- Rapid and irreversible hardening — Red Chalka soils upon drying
  ↳ constraint in groundnut, root crops — AP.
- addn of slow decomposing residues — paddy husk, coir pith — f.b. appropriate tillage
- Incorporn of powdered groundnut shells, paddy husk/straw or FYM at 5 $t ha^{-1}$ — 10 cm — 2 weeks before sowing kharif crops
- Efficiency — FYM 10 $t ha^{-1}$ > coir pith 20 $t ha^{-1}$ > powdered groundnut shell 5 $t ha^{-1}$ > gypsum at 4 $t ha^{-1}$ > paddy husk at 5 $t ha^{-1}$.

Crust

- Soils low in OM
- reduces exchange of gases
- Seed line mulch Tech — FYM 3 $t ha^{-1}$ or chopped wheat straw on seeded rows immedia. after sowing — maintain 3% ↑ soil H_2O in top 5 cm layer.

→ Straw mulch ↑ seedling emergence → ↑ yield

Shallow soils

- Insufficient soil volume— limits root growth and supply of H_2O and nutrients
- 10 cm high ridge on shallow soils (15-35 cm) – good for root growth.
- addn of clay or paddy husk.
- ridges and furrow on contour along with Vertiver barrier at an interval of 1 m. → ↓ runoff.
- ↑ maxm moist. retention.

Slowly permeable black soils

- Temporary waterlogg.
- Various tillage and land form treatments
  - Rid. and furr.
  - Broadbed and furrow (BBF)
  - (Raised and Sunken beds of diff widths) =

  effective.

  ↓

  Involves construction of raised beds alternating with sunken bed (similar to)

  ↓

  most imp on level land

  ↓

  widths depends amt of rainfall.
- crops susceptible to water log (soybean, chickpea, sorghum)

  ↳ raised beds.

  Those resistant – (rice) – sunken

  so, grown in same field.
- Double cropping during same year possible

Effects of modification of soil Phy. envn

Root growth

-

- Root zone temp and moisture – root functions
- optimum rhizosphere temp – cell division rapid – higher root proliferation – ↑access to H_2O and nut.
- warming ↓ water content of soil – limit enzyme and substrate diffusion.
- deep tillage / sub soiling of non plastic soils – continuous low soil strength.
- + straw mulching – moderate soil mechanical and hydrothermal regime.
- Integrated use of urea + Fym and deep till, sub-soil, straw mul

  ↓

  ↑ root mass density

  " length "

- Variations in soil water condition – affect root
- root hydrotropism – bending / growth of root in direction of ↑ moisture
- soil structure modification
- OC content ↓ in cultivation → ↓ stability of aggregates → ↓ root
- cultivation ↓ MBC → ↓ Root growth
- so, no-till → ↑ SOC
- In fine text – soil structure imp

  In coarse " – soil strength

Crop yield and Input Use Eff.

- Tillage ↑ crop yield → ↑ NUE, WUE
- Nutrient, H_2O, tillage – 3 key inputs – interact each other → ↑ crop yield, WUE

- Different in cropping sys, crop types, agro-climatic regions.
- Conservation tillage ↑ — due to moisture conservation → efficient fert utili.
- Appln of wild sage (Lantana camara) or eupatorium (Eupatorium adenophorum) to previous standing maize as mulch at recession of monsoon and incorp. of this — at sowing of rainfed wheat → ↑ crop yield of wheat
- Mulch modify soil hydro-thermal regime — ↑ NUE

Soil Bio.

- affects macro, micro flora and fauna — influences root growth.
- soil fertility dynamics.
- affected by tillage → ↑ or ↓ SOC.
- Earthworms – influenced by tillage.
- ↑ popn under no-till.
- Mulching with org. residues under consen. tillage ↑ popn earthworm
- Micro-organisms – tillage — disruption of fungi mycelia —
- alteration composition and substrate utilizatn of the microbial community in no-till.

Molecular structure of H_2O

- One mole (18 ml) of H_2O — 6.022×10^{23} molecules
- 1 cm^3 of liquid water at 20°C – 3.4×10^{28} molecules
- diameter – 3×10^{-4} µm or 3 angstrom
- 3 isotopes of H – ^1H, ^2H, ^3H
  3 " " O – ^{16}O, ^{17}O, ^{18}O
- H atom – +ve proton and –ve electron [$1s^1$]
- O atom – 8 protons (nucleus) – 8 electrons (surrounded) – 6 on outer shell
  [$8\ 1s^2 2s^2 2p^4$]
- ~~H atom~~
  outer shell of H lacks 1 e^-
- " " " O lacks 2 e^-
- strong intermolecular forces — due to electrical polarity
- O_2 atom shares a pair of e^- with each of 2 H atoms — overlap of 1s orbitals of H atoms with ~~by~~ 2 hybridized sp3 orbitals of O atom
- Vanderwaals radius of H – 1.2 Å
  O – 1.4 Å

  Covalent bond length – 0.965 Å
- H-O-H → 104.5° — near to tetrahedral arrangement of
- O atom's four possible sp3 orbitals – 109.5°.
- H-O-H distance – 9.65×10^{-5} µm
- arrangement of O_2 atom attracts e^- of 2 H atoms — H nuclei bare → local partial +ve charge
- O_2 – partial –ve charge – located in zone of unshared orbitals
- water molecules – no net charge – but electrical dipoles
- Dipole: — adsorption
  – dissolution of salts as ionic components of salts — greater affinity of H_2O mol. than for each other

- Free water - greater internal energy than ice
  - ↳ release of 80 cal (334 J) of energy → water → ice.
- ions - hydrated - heat of soln
- clay part - hydrated - heat of wetting
- Surface tension
- liquid air interface
- due to greater attraction of water mole for each other than for air above
- net effect :- inward force of H_2O molecules at surface
- plays imp. role in capillarity.

$$\Psi_t = \Psi_m + \Psi_p + \Psi_s$$

$$\Psi_w = \Delta\mu_w = \mu_w - \mu_w^0$$

μ_w — in arbitrary equilm state

μ_w^0 — soil water at standard state

$\Delta\mu_w$ — diff. in chemical pot of soil H_2O (Moisture Pot)

$$d\hat{G} = (\bar{v})_{T,\theta,n}\,dP + (\bar{S})_{P,\theta,n}\,dT + \left(\frac{d\hat{G}}{d\theta}\right)_{T,P,n} d\theta + \left(\frac{d\hat{G}}{dn}\right)_{T,P,\theta} dn + Mgh$$

$(\bar{v})_{T,\theta,n}\,dP$ — hydro pres

$(\bar{S})_{P,\theta,n}$ — ↳ constant pressure

$\left(\frac{d\hat{G}}{d\theta}\right)_{T,P,n}$ — matric sucto

$\left(\frac{d\hat{G}}{dn}\right)_{T,P,\theta}$ — Osmotic

Mgh — gravity

G = Partial molar Gibbs free energy

$\bar{v}$ = molar volume

$\bar{S}$ = molar entropy

m = molar mass

Adsorption H_2O on solid

- interfacial

Contd/–

- Sandy soil more conductive > clay – at low suction
  < – higher suction }

so, sandy soil absorbs H_2O rapidly during infiltration but then doesn't sustain evaporation process as can a clay soil.

EQUATIONS OF UNSATUR. FLOW

CONTINUITY EQN

- for a conserved substance (such as H_2O) – a sub. that neither created nor destroyed in soil – amount entering minus amount exiting a specified vol. of soil = change in H_2O content of same body.

– How to write a research Paper??

– Write like a reviewer and Editor
– Let someone else read it.
– Read it after a week.

For a reviewer
– New, significant or innovative work??
– Title accurate

IDEA ⟶ WRITE RESEARCH PAPERS ⟶ DO RESEARCH
ONLY STRUCTURE
(INFO TO BE REQUIRED)

PARTS
1. TITLE ⟶ 1 line 1000 readers ✓ Very important
2. ABSTRACT ⟶ 4 sentences 100 readers.
3. Intro — ½ page
4. Problem — ½ page
5. Table — ⅓ page
6. Figure — ⅓
– Findings — 1
details — 5 pages
Conclusion — 4 sentences
Full paper — 10 pages.

Title selection
– Don't be broad eg. Food production or global pop problem.
– If your topic is narrow — deal it with shallow way.
start with narrow idea

Abstract

- must have
  - line of introduction
  - objectives
  - most important results with actual values
  - an interpretation of results in terms of significance and possible implications
  - a line of conclusion.

Intro

- why did you do the work?
- what did you want to find out?

contain 4 parts:
- Background of the work
- A brief review of relevant literature
- Your hypothesis
- Objectives of the work.

Mat & Meth

- what did you use?
- " " " do?
- Don't interpret anything in this section.

Results

- Say what happened?

Discussion

- Most thoughtful
- What do my results mean and what are their implications?
- Why something happened and why things did not.

3 parts:
- Facts you have found
- your commentary on the facts
- theoretical implications of the fact

Table

- Tittle of the table must be complete

- Write title first → Methods — Results — Intro & discussion —
Abstract → References.
should convey only what you have written.

9/8/17 →

Physical properties

If BD ↓ → porosity ↑s

Fallow – no cultivation (∴ ↑s in BD/ ↑s it

→ Water stable → To hold the water in the soil.

→ NPK+FYM → ↑s soil physical parameters.

→ Aggregate ratio → [illegible] A / [illegible] A = Aggregate ratio.

1) Permeability (infiltration rate)

- porosity ↑
- → BD
- Hydraulic
- [illegible]
- H activity

Physical chemical

① pH → ē NPK+FYM

② EC → ē salt (electrical conductivity)

~~③ Cation exchange capacity CEC →~~

→ SOC → Soil organic carbon ↑ by NPK+FYM

→ FYM → ↑ ē [illegible]/polyphenol

→ Carbon content depends upon aridity (specially Temp)

→ Zerotillage/minimum tillage ↑s in OC (organic carbon)

→ Rice capturing atmosphere carbon + soil carbon

Lowland crop

- Weathering and soil formation – 26
- soil classfn – 27
- soil survey and mapping – 28
- Phy properties – 29
- soil water – 24, 25
- soil air and temp – 30
- soil erosion – 1
- Chemical comp. – 2
- soil colloids – 3
- soil acidity – 4, 5
- soil salinity – 6
- mineral nut – 5
- nitrogen } 6
- Phosp
- Potassium } 7
- secondary nutrients
- micronutrients } 8
- analyses
- soil fert evaluation } 9
- soil Bio & Biochem
- soil om – 10
- Fert, Manures and Bio. – 11
- soil fertili –
- soil and water pollution – 10
- soil management – for sustainable farming. – 12.
- land and soil indicators

Soil NE
Popn of India
Wheat Prod.
GDP

STCR

Pop. India – 1.252 billion
China – 1.3 billion
World – 7.4 billion

7.68 % of TGA
GDP

N.P.K

India Biodiversity meet 2016 – Oct 24-27
– Oct 10, 2016

BHU Managing Soil resource – 9-10 december 2016
– 15th Nov. 2016

WB science congress – 7-8 November

BHU climate change – 12-13 Nov.
– 25th Oct 2016.
– Full paper + abstract.

Telangana Prog – Dec-10-11, 2016
– Nov-10 (Full paper + abst.)

Sympos – BCKV – Nov-24-26

East zone meet – 8-9 Dec.
10 Nov.

Crop weed Sc – Jan-20-23
Nov 10.

ABC – 608 BIOCHEMISTRY OF ABIOTIC STRESSES (2+1)

(Theory)

Biochemical basis of abiotic stresses namely osmotic (drought, salinity), temperature, heavy metals, air and water pollutants. Synthesis and functions of proline and glycine betaine in stress tolerance interaction between biotic and abiotic stresses; stress adaptation.

(Prac) Reactive oxygen species and antioxidant potential under different systems of assay, assay of some antioxidative enzymes.

Assignments

(A1) : Physiological, biochemical & molecular basis of drought tolerance and its adaptation mechanism. (Satish)

(A2) : Physiological, biochemical & molecular basis of salinity (Madhu) tolerance and its adaptation mechanism, in case of various crops.

(A4): Physio, biochemical aspects of heavy metal toxicity in plants and its adaptation (Anand)

(A5) – Physio, bioch of air and water pollution on the plants and its effect on crop production. (Shiva)

(A6) – Function of proline and glycine betaine in stress tolerance. (Sisa)

(A7) – Combined effect of biotic and abiotic stress in diff. crops and interaction mechanism. (Gyanendra)

(A8) – Phy. bioch and molecular basis of submergence tolerance. (Nnaragesh)

(Bukanan) Plant Biochemistry & Molecular Biology.

– Advances in Stress Phy.

- Heat oil
↓
Bay leaves
↓
Onion (Brown)
↓
Tomatoes
↓
Salt - fry - moisture evaporates
↓
add garlic, ginger, turmeric pow, red chilli powder, potatoes
↓
add chicken
↓
Fry them well
↓
1/2 cups of H_2O
↓
half evaporate
↓
add another cup
↓
raw oil + turmeric oil + cumin powder + coriander powder -
30 sec
↓
Coriander